PERSON TO PERSON

The Living as a Christian Series

Basic Christian Maturity
Growing in Faith
 Steve Clark
Knowing God's Will
 Steve Clark
Decision to Love
 Ken Wilson
God First
 Ken Wilson
Sons and Daughters of God
 Ken Wilson
Growing Closer to God
 Tom Gryniewicz
Person to Person
 Jim Berlucchi

Overcoming Obstacles to Christian Living
How to Repair the Wrong You've Done
 Ken Wilson
Getting Free
 Bert Ghezzi

The Emotions
Facing Your Feelings
 Bert Ghezzi
The Angry Christian
 Bert Ghezzi
The Self-Image of a Christian
 Mark Kinzer
Living with a Clear Conscience
 Mark Kinzer
The Fear Factor
 Jim McFadden

Christian Character
Strength under Control
 John Keating
*How to Become the Person You
 Were Meant to Be*
 Peter Williamson
Growing in the Fruit of the Spirit
 John Blattner

Personal Relationships
Taming the Tongue
 Mark Kinzer

Bert Ghezzi and Peter Williamson
General Editors

Person to Person

How to Be Effective in Evangelism

Jim Berlucchi

SERVANT BOOKS
Ann Arbor, Michigan

Copyright © 1984 by Jim Berlucchi
All rights reserved

Published by Servant Books
P.O. Box 8617
Ann Arbor, Michigan 48107

Printed in the United States of America
ISBN 0-89283-164-2

Library of Congress Cataloging in Publication Data

Berlucchi, Jim.
  Person-to-Person.

  1. Evangelistic work.   2. Witness bearing
(Christianity)   I. Title.
BV3790.B456 1984   248′.5   84-10486
ISBN 0-89283-164-2

Contents

Living as a Christian

IN HUMAN TERMS, it is not easy to decide to follow Jesus Christ and to live our lives as Christians. Jesus requires that we surrender our selves to him, relinquish our aspirations for our lives, and submit our will to God. Men and women have never been able to do this easily; if we could, we wouldn't need a savior.

Once we accept the invitation and decide to follow Jesus, a new set of obstacles and problems assert themselves. We find that we are often ignorant about what God wants of us as his sons and daughters. For example, what does it mean practically to obey the first commandment—to love God with our whole mind, heart, and strength? How can we know God's will? How do we love people we don't like? How does being a Christian affect what we do with our time and money? What does it mean "to turn the other cheek?" In these areas—and many others—it is not easy to understand exactly what God wants.

Even when we do know what God wants, it can

be quite difficult to apply his teaching to our daily lives. Questions abound. How do we find time to pray regularly? How do we repair a relationship with someone we have wronged or who has wronged us? How do we handle unruly emotional reactions? These are examples of perplexing questions about the application of Christian teaching to our daily lives.

Furthermore, we soon discover that Christians have enemies—the devil outside and the flesh within. Satan tempts us to sin; our inner urges welcome the temptation, and we find our will to resist steadily eroding.

Finally, we must overcome the world. We are trying to live in an environment that is hostile toward what Christians believe and how they live and friendly toward those who believe and do the opposite. The world in which we live works on our Christian resolve in many subtle ways. How much easier it is to think and act like those around us! How do we persevere?

There is a two-fold answer to these questions: To live successfully as Christians, we need both grace and wisdom. Both are freely available from the Lord to those who seek him.

As Christians we live by grace. The very life of God works in us as we try to understand God's teaching, apply it to our lives, and overcome the forces that would turn us aside from our chosen path. The grace we need is always there. The Lord is with us always, and the supply of his grace is inexhaustible.

Yet grace works with wisdom. Christians must *learn* a great deal about how to live according to God's will. We must study God's word in scripture, listen to Christian teaching, and reflect on our own experience and the experience of others. Many Christians today lack this kind of wisdom. This is the need which the *Living as a Christian* series is designed to meet.

The book you are reading is part of a series of books intended to help Christians apply the teaching of scripture to their lives. The authors of *Living as a Christian* books are pastoral leaders who have given this teaching in programs of Christian formation in various Christian communities. The teaching has stood the test of time. It has already helped many people grow as faithful servants of the Lord. We decided it was time to make this teaching available in book form.

All the *Living as a Christian* books seek to meet the following criteria:

Biblical. The teaching is rooted in scripture. The authors and editors maintain that scripture is the word of God, and that it ought to determine what Christians believe and how they live.

Practical. The purpose of the series is to offer down-to-earth advice about living as a Christian.

Relevant. The teaching is aimed at the needs we encounter in our daily lives—at home, in school, on the job, in our day-to-day relationships.

Brief and Readable. We have designed the series for busy people from a wide variety of backgrounds. Each of the authors presents profound Christian truths as simply and clearly as possible, and illustrates those truths by examples drawn from personal experience.

Integrated. The books in the series comprise a unified curriculum on Christian living. They do not present differing views, but rather they take a consistent approach.

The format of the series makes it suitable for both individual and group use. The books in *Living as a Christian* can be used in such group settings as Sunday school classes, adult education programs, prayer groups, classes for teen-agers, women's groups, and as a supplement to Bible study.

The editors dedicate the *Living as a Christian*

series to Christian men and women everywhere who have counted the cost and decided to follow Jesus Christ as his disciples.

BERT GHEZZI AND PETER WILLIAMSON
General Editors

The Christian message is no opiate to send men to sleep, it is no comfortable assurance that everything will be all right. It is rather the blinding light which shows men themselves as they are and God as he is.

William Barclay.

ONE

The True "No Limit" Message

RECENTLY I RECEIVED an almost irresistible offer. I opened my mailbox one morning to find an attractively designed folder with this enticing offer: "How to be a no limit person." Of course, I opened the packet eagerly. The colorful brochure went on: "Yours for thirty days risk free . . . the blockbuster audio program from today's number one success-builder and best-selling author." Here was a six-cassette lecture series which promised to help me develop a "fresh, dynamic, you-oriented approach to career and personal life." Now I could "break the barriers to success," and "achieve super emotional and physical health," all for a mere pittance, $10 for 30 days with "no obligation." My every problem, frustration, delay, and failure, could be turned to my advantage. I could learn to live according to my maximum potential. This sounded like good news, indeed.

In fact, the author of this series was offering a glorious plan for personal success. Developed through his own life experience and research, he passionately wanted to pass on to others the best thing he had. He was inspired with "a purpose that shaped his own life—a mission to help people succeed." He was motivated by a consuming zeal to give others the best thing he had.

What is the best thing you have? Are you driven to share it with others? As Christians we should realize that we are the real "no limit" people. God has given us eternal life in Jesus Christ. We have received an entirely new nature through baptism in water and the Spirit. By God's power we have been transferred from the dominion of darkness into the kingdom of light, and we look forward to a heavenly banquet with God in our eternal home. We have received the magnificent power of God in our mortal bodies, far outstripping the human power and techniques flaunted in the brochure. Ours are new lives, characterized by power, joy, and the wisdom of our Creator. If the "no limit" author is consumed by a passion to "change the lives of millions of people," how much more should we, who have come to know the living God, desire to do whatever we can to change the world.

We can change the world, if we ourselves are living a full Christian life and are motivated to influence others toward a fuller relationship with Jesus. But why should a Christian be involved in evangelism?

I can think of at least five good reasons. First, Jesus commands us to spread the gospel. Second, evangelism results in a deeper union with Christ. Third, the world needs desperately to hear about Jesus. Fourth, telling others about Jesus is an exciting challenge that produces joy. Fifth, helping others choose for Jesus saves lives—eternally.

Jesus Commands Us

Consider, first of all, that Jesus commands us to spread the good news. Jesus' words at the end of Matthew's Gospel have been aptly described as the Great Commision. "Go therefore and make disciples of all nations, baptizing them in the name of the Father and of the Son and of the Holy Spirit, teaching them to observe all that I have commanded you (Mt 28:19-20). These were his last words to his disciples on earth. Jesus was not merely suggesting or encouraging them to spread the good news (the great suggestion); he was authoritatively directing them, and us, to "Go therefore." The true test of our love for God is our obedience to his will (Jn 14:21). Like it or not, if we are to love the Lord we must be personally committed to evangelism.

Deeper Union with Christ

Spreading the gospel also draws us into a deeper union with Christ. Just as we should integrate prayer, fellowship with other Christians, and the study of God's word into our lives, so too, should we be witnesses to others about Jesus. Most certainly, personal evangelism deepens our relationship with the Lord; it is a crucial life giving ingredient in the spiritual life. Through it we learn how to draw closer to God, rely on his help, and be led by his Spirit. As we take concern for others, our hearts are transformed into the heart of Christ who came to seek out and save the lost.

The World Needs the Good News

Consider also how desperately the world needs to hear about Jesus. War, pollution, crime, divorce, loneliness, murder, deprivation, and poverty constantly afflict the human species. Human solutions inevitably fall short. God's answer is life through God's only Son. No human being or society can be truly healthy apart from God. We who have been given new life in Jesus Christ, are the only ones who can offer hope to a dying world. The need of the world cries out to each of us—in our neighborhoods, families, schools, cities, and workplaces. We have only to open our eyes to see the desperate needs of those around us. Once we know their plight, how can we withhold from anyone, the only thing that will satisfy or free them?

Excitement, Challenge, and Joy

It is also true that the Christian life is the most thrilling, taxing, and fulfilling of all lifestyles. One could reasonably argue that the Christian faith is the only way to true self-fulfillment. A life lost for Christ is the only means to gain life.

When we evangelize others, we reach out to people we may otherwise ignore. We get involved with people's problems and concerns. We deal with the most profound issues of life. We fight in prayer for others; we persevere in meeting challenges; and we rejoice to see others experience more of God's love.

An Eternal Choice

We should always remember that men and women have a choice to make—between life and death. We can easily forget that spiritual reality. Michael Green says it this way:

According to Ephesians 2:1 men and women without Christ are dead. Their sin has cut them off from the life of God as effectively as death cuts a man off from the life of his friends. Though mentally, physically, and emotionally alive, people are spiritually dead until the life-giving elixir of the gospel begins to circulate through their veins. Society has lost its way.

Jesus Christ came to seek and save the lost (Lk 19:10). It is when we realize that our friends—our nice, decent friends—are lost without Christ that we long to help them and bring the good news to them.[1]

He goes on to say that there is simply no middle ground. Either we stand *for* Christ or *against* Christ. We either live under Satan's dominion or under the reign of God.

No matter how much we would like to think that the road to eternal life is wide and easily followed, the New Testament tells us otherwise. Jesus will have none of our compromising. We are being saved or lost, perishing or being born again. There is no middle ground.

An understanding of this reality can act as a tremendous motivation to evangelism. C.S. Lewis puts it frightfully well.

It is a serious thing to live in a society of possible gods and goddesses, to remember that the dullest and most uninteresting person you talk to may one day be a creature which, if you saw it now, you would be strongly tempted to worship, or else a horror and a corruption such as you now meet, if at all, only in a nightmare.

All day long we are, in some degree, helping each other to one or the other of these destinations.

It is in the light of these overwhelming possibilities, it is with the awe and the circumspection proper to them, that we should conduct all our dealings with one another, all friendships, all loves, all play, all politics.[2]

As sharers in God's nature and participants in this cosmic spiritual struggle, we hold a treasure in earthen vessels. Scripture likens us to the fragrance or aroma of Christ among those who are perishing. The question that confronts each of us is how we can personally contribute to this great process of salvation. Are there more than a chosen and gifted few who can effectively proclaim the gospel? What is the full message of the gospel? What are the attitudes and methods essential for effective witnessing? How can we overcome fear, embarrassment and the feeling of ineptitude we often experience in regard to sharing our faith?

Let's begin by considering what is involved in what I call everyday evangelism.

TWO

Everyday Evangelism

O VER THE LAST TEN YEARS, I have heard the conversion stories of many who have become Christians. I remember Barb's account of how she knelt next to her television one evening and surrendered her life to Christ in response to a media evangelist. A very gifted Methodist minister I know responded similarly as a child to Billy Graham. Another close friend of mine was changed radically at an evangelistic rally attended by signs and wonders. As he approached the stage in response to the minister's invitation to come forward, his eyes beheld a miracle. He actually saw someone's leg lengthen as the result of prayer. At the sight of this, he fell to his knees and gave his life to Jesus Christ. Another close acquaintance of mine turned from a very decadent life style one night at an evangelistic rally, by responding to the preacher's invitation.

These stories are examples of what has come to be known as "mass evangelism." Here we are talking about large group exposure to the gospel through some form of public preaching. God has worked mightily in such settings, and many people have come into the threshold of faith through them.

Another form of evangelism is called random evangelism. This form of witnessing is done by individuals or pairs of Christians, who offer a presentation of the gospel or a personal testimony to strangers. Sometimes Christians canvass neighborhoods, going door to door to evangelize people.

A Christian who engages in random evangelism is often praying and prepared to share the gospel at any time and in any circumstance, whether it be a locker room or on a plane flight. I know of one individual who actively testifies to players in informal basketball games at a local gym.

While random evangelism can be a good practice for Christians, it may not bear long-lasting fruit. However, it does sometimes result in remarkable and providential conversions. For example, I once purposefully and prayerfully chose to sit next to an elderly man on a twenty-minute bus trip. During that time I briefly shared with him about God's love. He was responsive and took my phone number as I got off. Later that evening he called my home and left a message with my wife that greatly startled me. He had determined to make that bus ride his last. His full and secret intention that afternoon had been to commit suicide as soon as he arrived home. Our brief conversation had dissuaded him, and he was calling to thank me. That experience taught me never to undervalue random evangelism, especially when we are being led by the God who knows the secret intentions of every heart.

In addition to random and mass evangelism, there are other sorts of methods. Neighborhood Bible studies are an increasingly popular method for helping people know and follow the Lord. Various forms of Christian entertainment (music, drama, and dance) have also been used effectively to communicate the gospel.

Another kind of evangelism is what I call everyday evangelism. Everyday evangelism involves influencing others toward the kingdom of God in our daily environments. Normally the process is most effective in situations where we have ongoing relationships with friends, neighbors, co-workers, relatives, or fellow students.

This kind of evangelism is seldom accompanied by signs and wonders and is done most frequently by people who are not extraordinarily persuasive, articulate, or charismatic. Often, the most effective witnesses are recently converted or renewed Christians whose enthusiasm makes up for lack of technical know-how.

At the heart of everyday evangelism is the

recognition of the importance of personal relationships in any kind of conversion process. Few people become dedicated Christians simply by hearing an inspiring message. Few converts are won solely through the distribution of tracts or by watching Christian television. In fact, most people respond favorably to the gospel through the personal influence of other Christians. This is particularly true when Christians show an interest and take initiative in the relationship. Very few non-Christians or nominal Christians seriously read or survey the Bible. It has often been said that the only Bible these people will see will be the lives of those Christians around them. Everyday evangelism assumes that most Christians can and will exert influence in their daily environments, reaching out to others with the life and love of Jesus Christ.

This kind of evangelism resulted, many years ago, in my own adult dedication to God. As a college student, I had turned my back on my Christian upbringing. The only time I entered a church was as a student protester. I slept on a pew one night with a few hundred other protesters who had marched on Washington.

I had actually gained some notoriety for my resistance to Christianity. I loved arguing with the very few Bible believers I knew, though I had little knowledge of what was actually being discussed. I had very little tolerance for religious types and was cynical about Christianity in particular. I was hardly an ideal candidate for conversion, especially through a church service or religious program.

Even so, I did come to know Jesus, thanks to the persistent, yet tactful, witness of some students in my dormitory. One of these students, Leo, seemed able to convert the unlikeliest prospects in the dorm. The lives of these new converts changed visibly and provoked a significant interest among the rest of us. These Christians began to share about the newfound reality of God in their lives. Today, years later, many of these men are now faithfully serving the Lord in a variety of occupations.

As I look back on those days, I am struck by the importance of personal relationships. Whether or not they knew it, the few Christian men living in that university dormitory were under close scrutiny by their fellow students.

Because Leo had been forthright and open about his love for God, I was curious to see if he were much different than the rest of us. Though I disagreed with his beliefs, I respected him for having serious convictions and I expected him to conduct his life with integrity. I was not disappointed.

As I watched him over a period of a few months, I noticed several impressive qualities. Unlike most of us, his life was well ordered and disciplined. His room was neat; he kept a consistent schedule; he was hard working and seemed to be in control of his life. Furthermore, I found it impossible to ignore his constant joy. His steady happiness made him standout in an environment that was often anything but joyful.

One could notice a sincere and attractive charity and generosity that characterized Leo's response to others. For instance, one evening I had a guest visiting from out of state. When Leo heard of his arrival, he brought his mattress into my room to accommodate my visiting buddy. To this day, I can remember the impact that selfless gesture had on me.

Leo was not one to criticize others or to complain even to the reasonable degree that I considered necessary for mental health. In conversations, where disrespect or negativity prevailed, he refrained from indulging. He would relate to others with extraordinary understanding and patience.

Leo was unrelenting in his desire to help me and others know and follow his Christ. We all knew he prayed for us. He would share with enthusiasm what God was showing him or how God was helping him. Whenever he returned from a church service or prayer meeting, he would tell his roommates and others what had happened. He would regularly invite and personally accompany different ones of us to these meetings, introducing us to his equally impressive Christian friends.

Over the course of eight months, four of the young men in this particular hall seriously committed their lives to Jesus. They had a great influence on the rest of us. Most of them couldn't hold their own in a theological debate. They were motivated simply to pray and pursue. The witness of their lives was indeed credible to their unbelieving acquaintances. They were the aroma of Christ to us—fragrantly drawing us and stirring us to consider the message of their Master. Their genuineness, tact, and personal credibility carried great weight. In the non-religious atmosphere of our dorm rooms, cafeteria, and lounges they were able ambassadors, by God's grace.

This example is neither rare nor dramatic; yet it shows the effectiveness of personal, everyday evangelism. Often, the sharing of faith by individuals in everyday relationships is only a smaller part of a larger orchestration by the Holy Spirit. A person might experience the action of God in several different ways: a period of personal crisis, invitation to a vibrant Christian gathering, reading a spiritual book, and so on. Nevertheless, everyday evangelism normally plays a critical role in capturing someone for Christ.

Everyday evangelism does not require years of theological training and expertise. You and I can do it. As you implement the principles of personal evangelism outlined in the next chapters, you will be increasingly able to help lead men and women further into the kingdom of God.

We might have the impression that effective evangelism requires extraordinary skill and extensive training. While training and gifts are helpful, we will do well to consider the words from an old hymn—"The Balm of Gilead": "If you can't preach like Peter, if you can't pray like Paul, go home and tell your neighbor, he died to save us all!"

THREE

Be Open, Be Natural

RECENTLY I HEARD A COMMENT that accurately reflected the attitude many Christians have about sharing their faith. It came from a dedicated young Christian woman who has had some success in evangelism. She said, "For years I was afraid of turning people off by aggressive evangelism. I was afraid of people's bad opinion of me. But now I find nearly 90 percent of the people I try to speak to about God will readily talk to me. Those who don't are free to say so, and we talk about something else. Often, listening to them, then becomes more important."

The foundation stone for everyday evangelism seems so simple and apparent that it hardly justifies mentioning. Yet many Christians don't realize that they can reach others in their daily environments simply by being open and natural about their Christianity. A simple willingness and readiness to share with others about our Christian lives is an essential ingredient in personal evangelism. This readiness differs from an aggressive showiness or pushy spiritual artificiality. Rather I am talking about the kind of openness which allows us to speak of the different aspects of our Christian lives naturally, as opportunities arise.

My dictionary lists sixteen definitions of the noun *open* and many fittingly describe this disposition, so important to effective personal evangelism. Consider, for instance: "uncovered or unprotected; exposed; not enclosed. Not secret or disguised; revealed; public. Without reserve or practice; frank, accessible."

I particularly noted the phrase "exposed, not enclosed." How often it seems that many Christians are decidedly "enclosed, not exposed!" Many people consider their faith a very private and personal matter, characterized by a kind of spiritual confidentiality. Jesus, on the other hand, called his followers "the light of the world," and told them not to hide their light under a bushel but to put it on a stand, where everyone could see it.

Unfortunately, some forms of aggressive style of evangelism can discourage people from openly sharing about the Lord. Such methods often help Christians overcome timidity, but, unfortunately, they can also produce a bombastic, programmed, or insensitive style of evangelism. A young Christian once told me about his involvement with this type of evangelism. He had carefully rehearsed a series of fifteen questions and responses designed to bring people to a choice for salvation. After being well drilled in the method, he successfully bulldozed his way over a few random unbelievers until he encountered an older man who was manifestly non-churchgoing. Each Sunday after the local church service, this man would pick up his wife at the church. One morning the young evangelist approached him and straightforwardly posed the critical starter question: "Mr. Adams, are you saved?" With corresponding directness, the man inched up to his face and shouted, "Shut up!" The flustered young evangelist panicked, realizing that this novel response had not been covered in the evangelism training manual. His instincts told him that he should approach this resistant victim some other time, some other way (maybe an anonymous note?).

The problems with many of the aggressive, programmed techniques are only too obvious. These approaches are artificial and often on a one-time-only basis, with random contacts. We use them on those with whom we have ongoing contact, we know that we will probably alienate them for good. A wise Christian will find many natural opportunities for witnessing to co-workers, neighbors, fellow students, and friends.

Even slight familiarity with aggressive and insensitive techniques can dampen our enthusiams for evangelism. Unfortunately, some Christians have reacted to this pushy style of evangelism by deciding to let their actions be their only witness for the Lord.

We must recognize that the witness of good deeds, though essential, is not enough for personal evangelism. The story of Robert helps illustrate this.

In the midst of an intense executive lifestyle, Robert experienced a profound change of life (a personal conversion) on a retreat weekend. His co-workers and subordinates noticed the difference immediately. Outbursts of anger, impatience, and cursing no longer punctuated his behavior. Instead, he displayed uncharacteristic contentment and patience in the face of pressing responsibilities.

Robert told no one about his religious experience, though he was now attending prayer meetings and avidly reading the Bible. Nevertheless, his change of behavior was intriguing, particularly to Pete, an accountant in the office.

Pete was so impressed by Robert's new-found reservoir of willpower that he tried to emulate Robert's model behavior—only to fail miserably.

About a year-and-a-half later, Pete was invited to the same kind of retreat weekend that had changed Robert's life. As a matter of fact, Robert was now a team member, leading discussion groups. To his surprise, Pete discovered the source of Robert's changed life. His immediate challenge to Robert was: "Why didn't you tell me about all this a long time ago? I would have given my life to God more than a year ago!"

Though his behavior was outstanding, Robert's failure to actually talk about what had happened to him short-circuited any evangelistic fruit he might have borne. After Pete's input, he decided to be more open about his Christian life. As a result, more fellow workers were influenced toward the kingdom of God.

The decision to be open about our Christian lives will, indeed, result in opportunities we would otherwise miss. Perhaps the best way to be open is in response to the needs and interests of others. That way we can customize the gospel for each person in order to make it most attractive.

Bill and Carol, for instance, live in a neighborhood on the outskirts of a major metropolitan area. Many of their neighbors are younger couples with small families. More than a few of the families have been torn apart by divorce. Other couples are struggling. As with many people, happy, successful family life seems to be escaping many of Bill and Carol's neighbors.

In contrast, Bill and Carol are succeeding quite well in raising their three children. As they consider how to evangelize their neighbors, it is clear to them that building a solid family life is a strongly felt need among their neighbors. As a matter of fact, a number of wives in the neighborhood complimented Carol on the behavior of her children. These comments have provided Carol with several opportunities to talk about the Christian approach to strong family life. Since she has identified herself as a Christian, the topic of Christianity and home life comes up naturally in her casual conversations with other neighborhood women. This has a slow, but steady influence in the neighborhood.

Bill and Carol have found an ideal opening for spreading the gospel in their neighborhood. They have been able to speak of their Christian lifestyle without cramming a spiritual message down anyone's throat. They have responded to the real concerns of their neighbors and established their own reputation as Christians. Their openness makes it easier for them to share and easier for others to relate to them. Though they have not yet won any converts they have managed to create a good deal of interest in their Christian faith. Some of their neighbors have begun to seriously evaluate their own family life. With this foundation, Bill and Carol can now decide on a more purposeful approach. They can focus on two of the most responsive couples, perhaps suggesting a four session group discussion on family life, based on the teachings of Scripture.

This kind of customizing of the gospel according-ing to the needs and interests of those around us is particularly helpful. The more prayerfully we can consider people's needs, the better able we will be to evangelize them. What do people talk about? How do they spend their time and money? What kinds of friends do they have? What motivates them? Asking these kinds of questions about people we see in an ongoing way is particularly important. By doing so, we minimize the chance of spoiling our witness through hasty or compulsive openness. It is not always wise to declare our spiritual colors at the outset of a relationship.

Even so, identifying ourselves as Christians is a fundamental and natural way of being open about our Christianity. In personal evangelism it is usually wise to give people time to adjust to the knowledge that we are Christians, rather than immediately launching into an explanation of the gospel message. If we begin by identify-ing ourselves as Christians, we will find that we have many opportunities later on to explain how we came to the point of commitment to Christ.

We can communicate the fact of our personal Christian commitment in any number of ways. Whatever we do, our identity as Christians should be communicated naturally, rather than as a stark or sudden statement of faith.

Sharing Our Experience

One of the best ways to tell others about God's love is by telling them our own experience of God at work in our lives. I often tell people about a remarkable series of jobs that the Lord has provided for me throughout the years. Natural circumstances have also provided me with the chance to tell others what God has done in my life after I was prayed with for a fuller release of the Holy Spirit. When we share on a personal level, about concrete situations, we straightforwardly attest to God's love. Moreover, being personal can encourage the hearer to be personal with us.

Conversely, doctrinal discussion nearly always generates debate, which is not usually helpful in personal evangelism. Generally, we should avoid it. This lesson was reinforced when I shared my faith with a man from India. The discussion began quite cordially about some theological differences between Christianity and Hinduism. But in a mere fifteen minutes we were literally nose to nose; he was shouting, his neck veins bulging!: "Jesus Christ is only a man!" At that point, I sensitively detected that our conversation had lost its former sweetness. I suspect our doctrinal encounter served only to enflame my friend's nominal Hinduism to a newfound fervor.

When we talk about our relationship with Jesus, we should share personally and naturally.

We should be ourselves as much as possible. Recently I read an article attesting to the effectiveness of the common earthworm as the best fishing bait available, better even than all the scientifically developed artificial lures in existence. Perhaps you can anticipate my point. We need not manipulate people or situations artificially. Evangelism happens best when we simply make use of the natural opportunities the Lord gives us. If we are open and aware, we will recognize the opportunities given us by the Holy Spirit.

Offering a Christian Perspective

Imagine that you are discussing the problem of political corruption with your barber. You might offer an observation like the following: "You know, Bill, it amazes me how widespread graft and bribery are, but I think the problem must go deeper. After all, deception and greed have been around since the human race began. All of us have been tempted, and some of us have even given in to the temptation to take advantage of others. Don't you think we need a bigger, more basic solution? This kind of approach is much more helpful than stark, dogmatic, or pious statements like "Well, the Bible says that all 'have sinned and fall short of the glory of God.'" Our comments should be designed to continue, not end, discussion. Normally, our remarks need not be explicitly religious, but they should reveal an underlying Christian perspective. For instance, to a problem at work you might respond: "The problem in our department involves more than just ignoring procedures. We all tend to gossip rather than to deal directly with the people involved."

Talking Freely about Christian Activities or Friends

When co-workers tell how they spent their weekend, it is natural to respond in kind. We can mention that we joined three other families for a picnic and canoe ride after church. It is good to be open about the fact that some of our activities are explicitly Christian. This is particularly the case if we are asked a question that can only be honestly answered by revealing that we were engaged in a spiritual activity—"what did you do last night, Mary?" "Actually, after dinner my husband and I went to a very interesting lecture." "Really, what was it about?" "A local author spoke at our church about how television can undermine family life. Did you know that the average American family spends twice as much time watching TV rather than relating to each other directly?"

We can share straightforwardly about our Christian activities in a way that is not pushy.

Discussion can be prolonged describing the content of the activity or its effect on us: "To tell you the truth, I was exhausted and crabby after dinner last night. The last thing I wanted to do was to go to a prayer meeting. But by the end of the night, I was glad I had gone. I felt refreshed by the music and the contact with other people. I slept well and feel great today."

The Christian activities that we tell others about or invite them to should be described sensitively and wisely. We should not go into too much detail describing things that would be unappealing or mysterious to a non-Christian. ("Oh, it was great! We interceded for two straight hours before our testimony and scripture witness.") Neither should we make it seem that we are so involved in Christian activities that we have no time for anything else. A non-Christian is not usually attracted to the idea of spending much time in such activities.

I have often heard Christians say, "I don't know anyone to evangelize." This comment reminds me of a missionary who was bound for an overseas mission. He was travelling on a huge ship which was transporting about two-hundred other missionaries two hundred tourists. As he considered the ratio of missionary to tourist, and the abundance of leisure time to socialize, he became excited about the potential of in-transit conversions. To his chagrin, however, he discovered that none of the other missionaries had even considered evangelizing the tourists. When he approached his fellow laborers about this, they were surprised at such a novel idea. They were thinking only of the foreign missionary field.

Taking stock of our daily relationships is an invaluable step in personal evangelism. Most of us have regular relationships with neighbors, merchants, relatives, friends, co-workers, and schoolmates. This is not to mention numerous random, short-term contacts that punctuate our daily routines. Praying and considering with whom and how we can effectively share about our faith sharpens our ability to be Christ's ambassadors right where we are.

FOUR

Building Bridges

ONE OF THE BEST WAYS of being open about our faith is to bring others into contact with fellow Christians. I call that bridge building. As individuals we lack all the human and spiritual resources needed to lead and help others into a full life in Christ. Only the body of Christ is sufficient for that task. In this chapter our focus is on how to put people in contact with a Christian environment.

We sometimes underestimate the importance of social groups and the potency of their influence on belief and behavior. Some psychologists subscribe to a theory spearheaded by the renowned psychologist, B.F. Skinner, that environmental factors exclusively shape human action. While this view wrongly excludes free will, it rightfully perceives that we are shaped to a great extent by our environment. In fact, our values, beliefs, clothing styles, and patterns of speech are powerfully influenced by the human circles in which we travel.

It is important, then, to use the life of the body of Christ to help win men and women more fully into the kingdom. This truth has foundational implications for the work of evangelism. We see its preeminence in the early church.

> And fear came upon every soul; and many wonders and signs were done through the apostles. And all who believed were together and had all in common; and they sold their possessions and goods and distributed them to all, as any had need. And day by day, attending the temple together and breaking bread in their homes, they partook of food with glad and generous hearts, praising God and having favor with all the people. *And the Lord added to their number day by day those who were being saved.* (Acts 2:43-47)

It is no accident that thousands were affected by a group of believers and were eventually added to their number. The Acts of the Apostles contains frequent examples of the influence of a body of disciples. Yet, because this kind of full body life is uncommon among modern Christians, it is often overlooked in the process of personal evangelism. Where it's working right, however, it provides a key link in helping others respond to Christ.

In fact, of the easiest ways to be open about our

Christianity is to simply invite others into our Christian circles. For example, a group in my town sponsors a weekly Christian professional men's breakfast. About one hundred men attend each week. The event is designed to to attract businessmen to the Lord and to support them in their Christian walk. Regular attenders invite non-Christians as well as Christian friends. Through this simple breakfast outreach, many business men have come into a deeper relationship with Christ. In this case, a simple invitation is the key step needed for personal evangelism. The individual Christian doesn't have the total burden of converting and discipling another, but can merely introduce him to a compelling Christian environment.

There are many examples of such spiritual bridge-building. It is well for us to take stock of the Christian environments we can use to help others in their Christian life. Perhaps our own home provides a powerful Christian witness. In his book *Disciples Are Made—Not Born*, Walter A. Henrichsen recommends that Christians invite potential or recent converts to their homes for meals and participation in family life. He recounts the impact of this involvement in his own life: "Bob W. Wheeler, a carpenter by trade, was the person who led me to Christ many years ago. One of the most significant things he did was to involve me in his family life. His home was my home. I always felt welcome. I cannot recall how many times I ate at his table, but I know I virtually ate him out of house and home!"[3]

We can invite others to share the warmth and fellowship of our church, prayer groups, or Bible studies. Not only will they receive spiritual nourishment, but they will also experience the power and vitality of Christian love. It was the firsthand experience of a large, joyous, affectionate group of Christians that motivated my search for spiritual renewal. I had never seen so much love expressed among so many different types of people. I concluded that they were either odd ducks or that they really had found some secret. I went on to search for and discover that secret.

If you give a little thought to bridge building, you will discover many such bridges. You might invite someone to lunch with your Christian friends, to a regular soccer game, to parties, barbecues, or concerts. The key is to provide a means of contact with other Christians. Such environments work best when you have already established natural relationships with other Christians yourself.

Natural activities and relationships are often the very best opportunities for extending invitations to outsiders. One group which I know of formed a softball team to compete in the city league. Most of the men were members of the same Christian group. They purposefully left open a few spots for some of their non-Christian friends. The Christian men had deep and affectionate relationships. Their love for one another was obviously expressed by their enthusiasm and mutual encouragement. One could quickly observe the absence of profanity and negativity among them. Moreover, they were good ball players.

The men played weekly, and most of their families were present at the games. Afterward they would gather at someone's home for an outdoor barbecue. The few non-Christian men along with their families participated regularly and were given special and warm attention by the Christian players, who were, in fact, praying for them and discussing among themselves how best to evangelize them.

The game and barbecues were not a pretext for speaking constantly about Christianity. Only infrequent remarks were made about spiritual matters. Yet the process strongly affected two of the men, who later joined a Bible study hosted by two of the Christian families. Eventually, these men became Christians. Later, they men cited the ball games and barbecues as the most influential ingredient in their own conversion. They were quick to perceive the joy and depth of their Christian teammates and were motivated by that observation as well as by the warm initiative of the Christian men. Vital kingdom relationships were instrumental in drawing these men into that same kingdom. It was not the work of a single man, but the work of a group of men. It was not the witness of a single life, but the corporate witness of the body of Christ. What a single worker could not do was done by men living and working together—giving witness to the new life which comes from Christ.

I have personally observed this principle of bridge-building many times in the past several years. I have found that one of the easiest and most natural ways of being open about my Christian life. None of us, including myself, is able to meet every need. I have found that the body of Christ is God's answer to the needs of many individuals. This resource is a key ingredient in personal evangelism.

If we have formed committed relationships with other Christians, it will be easy for us to introduce those we are evangelizing to key individuals and to invite them to various Christian activities. For instance, if you are evangelizing a physician, it might help to introduce him to a Christian physician you know. Whenever you recognize your own limitations in helping a particular person, try to connect them to someone uniquely able to help them. I remember a couple of instances in which I was trying to evangelize someone much older than myself. I found that it helped to arrange dinner and golf for my guest and myself with some older Christians.

What about evangelizing people of the opposite sex? This kind of evangelism can pose some own potential hazards. It can help to build bridges with someone of the same sex as the person you are evangelizing. With the help of other brothers and sisters, you can truly be "all things for all men" (and women).

If we want to bring others into contact with a larger Christian environment, it is important that we develop friendships with those we are trying to reach. No evangelist better demonstrated this principle than Jesus himself. "He ordained twelve, *that they should be with Him,* and that He might send them forth to preach" (Mk 3:14). He ordained them not just for service, but to be with him. Jesus ate, slept, traveled, and spent a great deal of personal time with his disciples. If our evangelistic efforts are to bear fruit, we must be committed to make friends and spend time with those we are trying to bring to Christ. Personal relationships in redeemed environments are the bread and butter of basic evangelism. Our aim is not to sell a product or to ensnare pagan victims, but to extend the "fragrance of the knowledge of him everywhere. For we are the aroma of Christ to God among those who are being saved and among those who are perishing, to one a fragrance from death to death, to the other a fragrance from life to life." (2 Cor 2:14-16) What is this fragrance if not the real affection and love that Christ himself has for men?

If we maintain friendships with people, we can continue to invite them into our circles, be available to offer advice, and recommend helpful books and tapes to them. Diligent follow-up insures our sensitivity to the working of the Holy Spirit. Our own faithful persistence offers a kind of spiritual protection from the strategic wiles of the devil. I make it a regular practice to stay in touch with people enough so that further invitations are not stilted and so that I don't offer advice in an ill-informed way.

Invitation, friendship, and follow-up when operating within the context of a larger Christian environment are normally indispensable in leading men and women into a full Christian life. An honest analysis of our relationships might motivate us to strengthen our own ties to a Christian environment. In personal evangelism, we must recognize that our evangelistic success depends critically on access to the body of Christ and to the head, Jesus.

FIVE

Praying Makes a Difference

A FEW YEARS AGO I asked an older Christian woman about the success of her backyard garden. "How do you get this kind of harvest?" I asked admiringly as I stood beside tall stalks of corn and top-heavy tomato plants. "Well," she said, and her face broke into a broad smile, "when I sow each seed in the spring, I just say, 'I plant you in the name of Jesus!' My neighbors are always jealous, but they don't believe in this sowing and praying business!"

As certainly as the power of prayer seemed to multiply that natural harvest, sowing and praying is mandatory for a spiritual harvest.

A friend of mine, currently head football coach for a major university, had great success in his previous assignment as defensive coordinator for the University of Michigan Wolverines. He orchestated a defense that refused to yield a touchdown in twenty-two consecutive quarters.

As impressive as his football success, his evangelistic catches are equally remarkable. When I once inquired about the secret of his spiritual reaping, he replied, "Someone once told me that a person can't come to Christ unless another Christian is praying for him. I believed that and have kept a list of people for whom I pray everyday."

I asked him how many people were on his list. "Well, I pray for quite a few," he said as he pulled out a typewritten sheet enclosed in plastic. "The hardest thing is remembering the names of all their children." My mouth fell open as I glanced at the list, dumbfounded. "You must have three hundred names on that list!" I stammered. "I used to," he replied. "Now it's about five hundred. For most people it is advisable to pray for fewer than ten individuals on a regular basis. Obviously, this man had a gift for more.

People who are serious about reaching others with the love of God in Christ are always serious about prayer too.

A former college professor who has won many people to Christ once told me of an experience he had while lecturing one day. In the middle of his presentation to a large class, the Holy Spirit suddenly called his attention to a student near the front. The professor realized that the Lord was particularly interested in drawing this young man to himself.

"I began to pray for him. I told the Lord that he needed to bring that young man more directly onto my path. Soon afterward, guess who showed up at my office, handed me a slip, and said, "You've just been appointed my faculty adviser?" Within a short time, the professor was offering more than academic advice, and the student made a huge change of life, turned from his sin, and became a fervent Christian. This change, initiated by the Holy Spirit, was wrought by the teacher— sowing and praying.

God will respond in unexpected ways as we pray for others. Through our prayer, God can begin to stir up a deeper desire for his life in the hearts of those for whom we are praying. He will alter circumstances, provoke hidden needs, and even reveal himself to someone quite independent of a human agent. I recently received the following account from a woman who prayed for her family.

When I visited my family over Thanksgiving vacation, I became very concerned about people's personal lives. While I was asking the Lord to help them, I sensed him saying, "You know, Meg, I could just step in and patch things up in these people's lives, but in a few months they they would be in other situations they couldn't handle because they don't know me or turn to me. Pray, instead, for their salvation. Then I can give them what they need to deal with anything."

I replied by saying, "Lord, I've known these people all my life and they're not going to change. They're not the religious type." As soon as I said this, I realized my presumption and repented for my lack of faith. I asked God for faith to believe my family would change, and I began claiming their salvation and praising God for changing their lives. During the next three work days, I used my lunch breaks to pray for my family rather than for eating lunch.

About a week later my sister called and told me that the funniest thing had happened. That week she had had the same dream on two successive nights. She dreamt she died, but when she met God, she knew she wasn't right with him and wouldn't be able to stay with him. As a result of the dreams, she worked through some problems relating to her husband and both of them began attending church again regularly.

A month later, my father, who hadn't set foot inside a church for fourteen years, was piloting an airplane on a short, solo flight. The engine quit in mid-air, and the plane crashed. Though the plane was completely destroyed, my dad opened the cockpit door and stepped out without a mark on him. You can imagine how this affected him. Though he isn't one to talk about his beliefs, he went back to church the next Sunday and has attended nearly every Sunday since for the last two years. His personal life has straightened a good deal, and even though the problems haven't completely vanished, he is now in a position to receive help from the Lord.

This woman's prayer was effective for several reasons. First, she was motivated by genuine love. Her intercession for her family resulted from her concern for them. Second, she was not only mindful of her family's dilemmas but sensitive to the Holy Spirit. Rather than praying according to her own assessment of the situation, she was able to be directed by God to pray according to his purposes. This is critical. We can become so focused on our own concerns for others that our petitions may be off center. The Holy Spirit wants to shape and inspire our prayer according to God's will for the person or situation. As we pray according to the mind of God, his power is released in the lives of others.

During certain times and seasons, God wants to mobilize our prayer in special ways. For instance, Meg was inspired to focus her intercession with considerable intensity for a short period of time. In particular, she did some fasting and prayed at length for three days. Quite dramatically, God answered her prayers almost as soon as they were spoken.

Concerted or intense intercession, inspired either by a sense of spiritual urgency or by natural circumstances, is one way to pray for others. Though we will not always experience the kind of quick and dramatic results that Meg did, we can be assured of God's reliability and responsiveness. It is not difficult to imagine the good pleasure that the Heavenly Father experiences at the earnest and fervent petitions of his people. Stronger, more intense spiritual assaults are needed in our warfare against Satan himself. "For we are not contending against flesh and blood, but against the principalities, against the powers, against the world rulers of this present darkness, against the spiritual hosts of wickedness in the heavenly places" (Eph 6:12).

We cannot underestimate the importance of prayer. Our persistent prayer is a potent spiritual force opposing the work of Satan and opening the door for others to respond to God. Our prayer not only does people good, but it fosters our love for them and helps us align our own perspective with that of our heavenly Father.

Recently I was annoyed and impatient with a man I was trying to help. I had invited Brian to a regular Christian meeting and maintained a good deal of personal contact with him. For some reason, in the midst of what had seemed like good spiritual progress, he stopped coming to the meetings and refused to return my phone calls to his office. My annoyance grew into a subtle resentment at what seemed like a calculated retreat on his part. Even so, I stepped up my phone calling, but without result.

In the midst of this exasperation, I sensed the Holy Spirit trying to set my thinking right. As I paused to listen to his counsel, the prescription was clear: "Quit calling. Start praying." With an embarrassed reluctance I began to pray for Brian daily, and at some length. As I prayed, I recognized and repented of my impatience. Instead of being resentful, I began to be more compassionate and relaxed about the situation. My own human perspective diminished, and God's perspective began to take hold.

During this time, I told the Lord I would take no action other than prayer, unless and until he directed me to do otherwise. About six weeks later, I felt directed to call Brian. Once again he was unavailable, so I left a message. The next morning, he called back, explaining his absence and expressing his desire to resume contact. Since then, he has made steady progress with the Lord. For my part, I am trying to pray more and interfere less!

This experience taught me a lesson about the importance of praying for those we are trying to serve. Prayer can be hard work. It will not always seem inspired. Just as we experience dry times in praise and worship, so, too, intercession will often seem difficult and unfulfilling. Only by the grace of God, the exercise of wisdom, and the help of others can we be faithful in praying for others. A few practical tips can help us be faithful to intercession:

Set Aside a Time and Place

As in any natural activities, practical planning and implementation is much more likely to produce success than irregularity and spontaneity. While we should be open to inspiration, a careful plan for intercession is wise. The plan could vary greatly depending on our circumstances, natural disposition, and God's design. Some people intercede for fifteen minutes at a time, three times a week. One homemaker I know has designated certain areas of her home and certain regular tasks for intercession. For instance, whenever she folds laundry, she prays for her sister and brother-in-law. When cleaning her son's bedroom, she consistently prays for another person. Some people intercede for others while they jog. (I am afraid I don't have the gift.) Others pray while commuting to or from work. Whatever your personal inclination, it helps to establish a regular time and place for prayer.

Methods of prayer can vary greatly as well. One

person might recite a fixed prayer of petition or pray for a set amount of time per individual. Some people maintain a prayer list of individuals for whom they regularly pray. Others might pray the same psalm or a prayer from the New Testament (see Eph 3:14-19). We should not be inflexible in our method, but open to the Spirit.

Establish Reasonable Goals

We should be familiar enough with our prayer capacity that we don't overtax our spiritual muscles. It is better to apply steady spiritual pressure against the enemy for a few people than barely to scratch the surface for scores of individuals. The one who is faithful in a little will be given more.

Join with Others

"Again I say to you, if two of you agree on earth about anything they ask, it will be done for them by my Father in heaven. For where two or three are gathered in my name, there am I in the midst of them" (Mt 18:19-20). This remarkable promise can most certainly be applied to intercession. Two or three is not so awesome a number that it cannot be met with ease. However, it is spiritually significant enough to command an incredible commitment from God himself.

Praying with others is not only more effective on a spiritual level, it is also helpful on a natural level. Encouragement, inspiration, and accountability help us to remain faithful in prayer. Two years ago I agreed with twelve other men on a seven-day prayer contract. We each agreed to pray for thirty minutes daily for a particular non-Christian man. On more than one occasion I finished my prayer just before midnight, but I was faithful each day because of the commitment I had made to the others. Moreover, I was inspired to know that six hours of intercession were offered daily by the group. I might add that the man we prayed for has taken noticeable steps toward the kingdom of God.

Pray with Patience

Patient prayer is potent prayer. Augustine's mother, Monica, is known for her unyielding persistence in prayer for her worldly son. She prayed with tears for many years for Augustine, though she saw no evidence of his conversion. Eventually her persistance was rewarded, and her prayers were of immense benefit to the whole Christian people.

We can be strongly tempted to give up when we don't see quick results. In the spiritual realm, instant results are rare, and we are well-advised to prepare for the long haul, remembering that we are moved by faith and not by sight. "Now faith is the assurance of things hoped for, the conviction of things not seen" (Heb 11:1). Furthermore, God approves of this kind of faith. "For by it the men of old received divine approval" (Heb 11:2).

I would venture a guess that maintaining this kind of faith over a long period of time is one of the greatest tests that faces us in evangelism. This is especially true the closer the relationships. Praying for family members, for instance, can challenge our faith to the limit. May we never forget that our Lord is great, powerful, and able to do all things. "God is not a man, that he should lie, nor a son of man that he should change his mind. Does he speak and then not act? Does he promise and not fulfill?" (Nm 23:19)

If we prepare ourselves for a long fight that will require hardy and enduring faith, we will be better equipped to meet and prevail over the inevitable storms of spiritual resistance. The cost is high but the prize is great. Imagine the joy of one day viewing even one soul who has been vindicated in the sight of God largely as the result of your prevailing and patient prayer.

Pray for Laborers

Jesus' perception of the harvest of souls for the kingdom of God seems to indicate that the biggest problem involves the lack of harvesters. "When he saw the crowds, he had compassion for them, because they were harassed and helpless, like sheep without a shepherd. Then he said to his disciples, 'The harvest is plentiful, but the laborers are few; pray therefore the Lord of the harvest to send out laborers into his harvest.'" (Mt 9:36-38)

Moved by compassion for the lost sheep of his generation, Jesus assessed the situation as a labor crisis—a severe shortage of harvesters. He thus instructed his disciples specifically to pray for laborers.

Our situation today is the same. The Lord of the harvest has explicitly exhorted us to pray for laborers. For many years, Christians have obediently made this their own petition. We should also make this our prayer.

Through the years I have hoped to win many close friends and family to the Lord. However, God has made it clear that in certain cases I am not to be his chosen instrument. Instead, my part is to pray that God will send someone else to represent his case. This awareness relieved me of a misleading sense of responsibility to preach and reminded me of my God-given responsibility to pray. This prayer for harvesters is one we should all pray frequently.

SIX

Evangelizing Relatives and Friends

MOST CHRISTIANS ARE ESPECIALLY concerned for the spiritual welfare of those closest to them. All of us have close friends and relatives who either do not know the Lord or whose experience of the Christian life is inadequate. Understandably, these are the people who come to mind first as we consider reaching others with the full gospel.

Close relationships often prove ideal for telling others about the good news. This was certainly evident in the New Testament. For example, after Andrew was called by Jesus, he immediately went to his own brother, Simon Peter. "The first thing Andrew did was to find his brother Simon and tell him, 'We have found the Messiah' (that is, the Christ). Then he brought Simon to Jesus." This pattern has been frequently relived throughout the centuries, as brothers, sisters, fathers, mothers, and various relatives and close friends have helped introduce their kinsmen to the Messiah. Because of our knowledge of and love for those who are close to us, we can often be influential in their spiritual betterment.

On the other hand, we can face the greatest challenge when it comes to evangelizing those close to us. Our past relationships may have been fraught with difficulty, tension, or wrongdoing. Bad patterns of relating may have become habit over time.

No one is more familiar with our weaknesses, faults, and problems than our relatives and close acquaintances. They can more readily perceive gaps between our Christian convictions and our daily behavior. They might also be the people who can most readily provoke our worst behavior.

The closer we are to someone, the more difficult it is for us to be objective about our relationship with them. Our view of the other person can easily be clouded by our own emotional reactions, and perhaps by too frequent contact. Familiarity not only tends to breed contempt, but also a certain obliviousness to the dynamics of the relationship.

Christians are often most eager for the conversion of those they know and love well. This eagerness is both natural and good but it can develop into a pushiness or impatience that is harmful. Because of the close relationship, we are also more aware of their shortcomings and more eager for them to change. Because these people are so important to us we are particularly grieved and concerned, especially where serious sin or disorder exists in their lives.

An effective witness to relatives and friends requires special wisdom from the Lord. All of us can think of a few well-intentioned but miscalculated and ill-fated evangelistic efforts like the ones that follow.

Ted, a lukewarm Christian all his life, had a life-changing encounter with Jesus. He made *every* effort to speak about it to his immediate family. While appreciating his sincerity, his adult brothers and sisters grew increasingly irritated at his "smug self-righteousness." He became something of a family joke and alienated relatives by his regular preaching.

Ken, a recent convert, visited his older brother in San Diego, hoping to influence him for the good. Accompanied by a Christian friend to a "worldly" party hosted by his brother, Ken watched with dismay as his zealous colleague abruptly stopped the party to lecture to the whole group. Though it was not his own error, Ken later concluded that his friend set back his relationship with his brother at least ten years.

Larry, a Wall Street stockbroker and father

of three small children had a dramatic conversion which immediately results in a rapid change of lifestyle. He now regularly carries a Bible, quoting passages to his wife with unabashed enthusiasm. To his shocked disappointment she digs in her heels, resisting his "fanaticism."

With great eagerness, Carol returned home during a break in her college semester. She could hardly wait to tell her parents of her recent experience of the Holy Spirit. Unfortunately, her mother dismissed her daughter's new-found experience and seemed aware only of the mud Carol kept tracking onto the living room carpet.

I conclude that while close relatives are excellent candidates for person to person evangelism, they are also frequently manhandled by their own more zealous friends and relatives.

One Christian woman recently informed me of the Lord's directive to her regarding her family's conversion. It went something like this: "Yes, Nancy, I do want to reach your family, but I have not chosen *you* as the instrument." In this counsel, she recognized more clearly than ever some problems in her relationships with key family members that could undermine her usefulness in imparting the gospel to them.

Step One: Start with the Heart

A good rule of thumb in close relationships is to aim first at affecting the other person's heart. The closer the relationship the more critical this principle. Those who know us well will pay particular attention to positive changes they see in our behavior or in the way we express concern for their needs. Beginning with the heart usually means that we don't start with a direct spiritual message. Instead, our efforts are channelled into serving and showing consideration to others.

Love expressed in good deeds speaks loudly and clearly. This is even more the case when the love we express is the kind of love that others *can experience as love*. Nancy's words about God's love were overshadowed by her negligence in tracking mud into her mother's home. Larry, the father of three, could probably have reached his wife more effectively by frequent thoughtful acts than by regularly quoting Bible passages. In each case, working on another's heart is more persuasive than direct witnessing.

Keith Miller, in the book *A Taste of New Wine*, describes his efforts to lead his wife to an experience of Christ. He used some very direct means, actively preaching to her and inviting her to meetings she didn't enjoy. The more she resisted, the more desperate he grew. He was ready to do "anything" to show her he was a new person and to have her join him in his spiritual walk.

A long-standing point of tension in their marriage had revolved around a rather mundane item—the wastebasket. His wife's father had always emptied the wastebasket in her family. The opposite was true in Keith's family. The only thing his father ever did with the wastebasket was help fill it.

Soon after the honeymoon "the invisible battle lines are drawn across the soul of a marriage and the siege begins . . . so the wastebasket in the kitchen became the first article of furniture in the soul of our marriage, which had to be stepped around almost daily in our relationship."[4]

Years later, desperate for his wife's conversion, Keith promised that he would do *anything* to convince her that he had really changed. Suddenly his glance fell upon, you guessed it, the hated wastebasket. "No, Lord," he groaned quietly to himself, " *Not* the wastebasket. Take my income, anything." Suddenly, he knew with clarity of at least one way to show his love in a way his wife would experience as love.

Without any fanfare or comments, he simply initiated the daily routine of taking out the wastebasket. Within a few weeks, his wife committed her future to Christ. This simple act had communicated a great deal to provoke the conversion he had tried for so long to establish in more direct ways. In this intimate relationship, the most effective strategy was to affect her heart first.

Two principles are striking in this humorous and true account. One, carrying the trash was a concrete act of service that was greatly appreciated by the receiving partner. Clearly, she perceived it as an act of love for her. Her husband could have chosen any number of more heroic ways to serve her. He could have prayed for her two hours a day. He could have brought home flowers regularly. He could have scrubbed the kitchen floor for her. The act of removing the wastebasket was particularly potent, however, because *she experienced it as love.* It was a simple gesture with great symbolic meaning, beautifully customized for her perceived need. It was love on her terms, not his.

Second, this small act signalled a positive change in the husband. Something had obviously happened to him that caught his wife's attention and won her favor. It was the kind of change that speaks loudly and favorably in a close relationship. A change of behavior that is perceived positively can penetrate the heart.

Step Two: Move to the Head

If we start with the heart, we can at least have a reasonable basis on which to share the gospel more directly. Assuming that one's heart has been touched, we can more effectively begin sharing verbally about the Lord the more we can speak from our personal experience, as opposed to preaching, the better.

I remember with regret the unfortunate series of evangelistic moves I put on an old friend shortly after my spiritual reawakening. While demonstrating a limited amount of redeemed behavior, I vaulted into step two with gusto. After confronting him about some questionable morals, I took an hour to explain the real theological meaning of the atonement. Moving at a breakneck pace, I asked him two days later why he didn't go to church any more. At that point he began to show signs of defensiveness to my inquisitiveness and lecturing. Couldn't he see I was concerned about his spiritual welfare?

Unfortunately, my efforts were premature. Had I laid a better foundation—paying attention to his needs, listening to him, showing respect for him—step two would have made its important contribution. Moreover, I would have done better to have shared more personally what Christ had done in my life rather than to preach and browbeat him with theological truth.

At some point we can expect that Jesus will give us opportunities to speak of him. The second step, speaking of Christ, is an important one. Faith comes by hearing the word of God. When aptly spoken, our personal testimony can have significant impact upon those close to us. I recall the contact I had with another one of my close friends, who eventually received Christ. Because I had handled him better in the first stage than my other friend, and concentrated on sharing my personal testimony with him, my efforts had a strong, positive impact. Shortly after his conversion, he wrote an account of this change that was published in a Christian newsletter. The following excerpt refers to his contact with me in that process of conversion.

In 1971 a close friend told me that his entire life had been transformed as a result of giving himself completely to Jesus Christ and experiencing a release of the Holy Spirit in his life. As he spoke to me about Jesus, I felt angry because I perceived him as being naive, and I felt that he had compromised his intelligence in order to have the emotional security of "believing in God." I was upset because I could see how his life had changed, and I was envious. My friend was genuinely full of love and joy. His faith in the Lord was strong and solid because he experienced the Lord working in his life in daily and practical ways.

Through this and other conversations that I had with Christians, the Lord began to soften my heart toward Him.

In this second stage, our aim is not so much to draw forth a response from the person but to communicate some truths about God and his call to us. At this point we are sowing the seed of God's word in the well-prepared soil of the heart. We should not normally be addressing areas that need to change in the person, nor should we tell them how to live more fully for God. These things can come at a later point. Our goal as we move from the heart to the head is to impart God's truth for the particular situation.

This approach takes faith. We must believe that the truths of God have, in themselves, the power, when planted, to bring forth life. God's word has creative power, and we can depend on its ability to produce.

As we share some aspects of the Christian life with close relatives in this second stage, we should *personalize* and *customize* our comments as much as possible. For this reason, some form of personal testimony is recommended. Theological truth can be readily debated. It almost invites confrontation. Personal sharing, on the other hand, is hard to argue with, and when well substantiated by our behavior, it tends to be convincing.

Close friendships offer us the advantage of greater familiarity. Often, we know the other person's religious background and experience. We can anticipate objections and fears. Perhaps we are acquainted with particular misconceptions they hold about Christianity. All this information should help us customize spiritual truth for their benefit. Perhaps certain material should be stressed and other elements avoided.

For instance, a close friend was raised in a church that stressed morals and legalism. There was a certain coldness in relationships and inhibition in worship. God was not identified as a personal father but as a scrutinizing, intolerant judge. This imbalanced religious background created both a misconception of Christianity and a subsequent rejection.

In this case, my knowledge of this individual enabled me to highlight the person of Jesus, his forgiveness, his compassion, his desire to know and be known. I did not begin by proclaiming the ten commandments but emphasized the truths so obviously absent in my friend's background. I also tried to speak directly to the inadequate or misleading notions of God as a tyrant and Christianity as oppressive.

Step Three: The Will

With the right preliminaries in a well-established and close relationship, it is entirely fitting for a Christian to appeal to another's power of intention and decision, to the will. The will is indeed a private domain, created and respected by

God himself. It is here that we all make countless decisions, some with enormous consequences. The will is a primary contact point with God, the place where one can freely choose to respond to the Lord's call.

It has been said that "a man convinced against his will is of the same opinion still." There is a truth here that needs to be acknowledged by Christians eager for their loved ones to make the ideal spiritual choices. To manipulate or pressure others to decide more fully for the Christian life is seldom if ever effective—particularly in a society which so strongly values independence and freedom of choice.

Nevertheless, we should appeal to the will of others. The apostle Paul persuaded, cajoled, warned, and entreated his listeners to be reconciled with Christ. The prophet Ezekiel was warned that the blood of his brethren would be on him if he neglected to warn them of God's decrees.

If the heart and the head have been prepared, the will can be appealed to at the right time. The right time is the timing of the Holy Spirit. Coordinating our efforts with his initiative is critical for success.

A young woman I know had been praying for her brother for some time. He was not a Christian and her primary strategy was to demonstrate love with persistent prayer and some verbal witness. This proved worthwhile and resulted in the following incident:

> Later that winter, my seventeen-year-old brother initiated a conversation with me. "I was laying in bed the other night," he said, "and I was just sort of thinking about my life and I started talking to God. Not that I do that all the time or anything, but I told God that I had always been the nucleus of my life and that things weren't working out too well. So I told him I wanted him to be the nucleus of my life from now on, and boy, have I ever felt *great* since I told him that!" We spent the next hours sharing and praising God together.

At this point, when the Holy Spirit was making a move, she was able to appeal to his will by encouragement and support. Encouragement from a Christian who is close at hand at these times can be ideal, provided that a good foundation has been laid.

The appeal to the will can come in many varied forms. If someone is particularly responsive and the timing is right, we might call that individual to make a significant choice for Christ. On the other end of the spectrum, we might merely extend an invitation to a Christian event. The array of possibilities and circumstances is broad. The key thing to understand at this stage is that we are calling for some kind of response. It is not enough to work on someone's heart and head and never call forth a response. On the other hand, it is unwise to appeal to someone's will if we have neglected the preliminaries.

These three stages are by no means an ironclad formula for evangelistic success with those who are close to us. Nor is it easy or necessary to isolate each step in the sequence. Often the three steps will intermingle. This simple three-step recommendation recognizes that there is a certain rhyme and reason for dealing with people we know well.

SEVEN

The Gospel
and Good Works

M ANY OF US REMEMBER the peace movement
in America during the late 1960s and
early 1970s. It was fueled to a large degree by the
Vietnam war. Many young people simplified and
sentimentalized the notion of peace. The Beatles,
for instance, made a lot of money on a song
whose main message was "all we are saying is give
peace a chance." Shortly afterward they broke up,
the result of some irreconcilable differences.

The peace movement was strongest on college
campuses. Many students were socially conscious
and idealistic, determined to change the world
they lived in. Lambasting the greed and tyranny
which characterized the "capitalist system,"
thousands of strident, naive student protesters
vowed to shape a brave new world.

I remember joining the volunteer staff of a
student newspaper on campus in my effort to
change society. I was enthralled to be in the

company of young, bright, selfless idealists working unitedly against the ills of the world.

Within a short time, however, I was unnerved by what I saw in these selfless idealists. Jealousy and backbiting were common among various editors. Many of the staff seemed to have fragile and inflated egos. Arguments flared quite easily, gossip was common, selfishness rampant. My bubble began to contort—then it burst. The very problems we were seeking to solve worldwide flourished in our midst! How empty all the words and editorials about greed and injustice seemed to me, as I considered the vivid testimony of our own lives.

Soured and sobered by this experience, I was motivated to look to elsewhere for the answers to these very basic human problems. Even my untrained eye could see that the validity of one's message is best judged by the witness of one's life. Talk is cheap but action costly.

Just as the obvious selfishness of many of my idealistic colleagues quenched my zeal for the peace movement, the actions of some Christians arrested my attention.

I was impressed by the thoughtfulness and concern that was regularly demonstrated by members of a local Christian group. One young man whom I had just met invited me over to his apartment for a fine meal and gracious hospitality. Another Christian acquaintance volunteered to type a paper for me during a time when I was particularly busy. These actions, plus many more, were instrumental in a spiritual change that began to take place in my life. I am certain many have been drawn into a new or fuller Christian life, largely by the loving actions of other Christians toward them. Conversely, many have not been won, because they have yet to personally experience real Christian love.

This principle of love is broadly recognized as an important tool of persuasion. To a significant degree, the membership growth in various sects and cults can be attributed to the warmth and love initially extended to outsiders. Even the most secular activities and causes can attract people to them by the demonstration of love and concern. Though this kind of love is often shallow and fleeting, it can attract enough to fulfill its purpose. A highly touted college athlete once told me, "Boy, that coach was so nice and friendly when he recruited me—smiling, attentive, gracious. What a change after I was signed and at practice! He turned real mean and nasty—quick!"

Genuine Christian love differs from the world's version, in at least two ways. First, it is directly rooted in the only true source of love for the world—the love of Christ. "In this the love of God was made manifest among us, that God sent his only Son into the world, so that we might live

through him. In this is love, not that we loved
God but that he loved us and sent his Son to be
the expiation for our sins." (1 Jn 4:9-10) We are
now able to love others effectively because we
have received the momentous, empowering,
eternal love of God Almighty. "We love because
he first loved us" (1 Jn 4:19).

Second, Christian love rightly directs its recip-
ients towards man's greatest good. The apostle
Paul showed through his actions and his words
the genuine love that compelled him to serve
both believers and non-believers. This love was
directed toward the highest, most noble aspirations. To the church in Philippi he wrote:

> For God is my witness, how I yearn for you all
> with the affection of Christ Jesus. And it is my
> prayer that your love may abound more and
> more, with knowledge and all discernment, so
> that you may approve what is excellent, and
> may be pure and blameless for the day of
> Christ, filled with the fruits of righteousness
> which come through Jesus Christ, to the glory
> and praise of God. (Phil 1:8-11)

Paul wanted their love to abound not simply
because it would win more converts, good as that
goal might be, but so they could be pure and
blameless, filled with the fruits of righteousness.

The ultimate purpose of love is for "the glory and praise of God."

Love is cited frequently in the New Testament as the highest virtue. We are told that it is greater than all gifts, knowledge, and ability. We are charged to make it our aim in all relationships—with Christian and non-Christians alike. It is the basis for Christian unity—a sign to a lost world that they may believe. Jesus thus prays for his disciples, "that they may become perfectly one, so that the world may know that you have sent me" (Jn 17:23).

Showing love to others is not an evangelistic ploy or strategy. The love that Christians have even for their enemies is a stamp of their sonship:

If you love those who love you, what credit is that to you? For even sinners love those who love them. And if you do good to those who do good to you, what credit is that to you? For even sinners do the same. And if you lend to those from whom you hope to receive, what credit is that to you? Even sinners lend to sinners, to receive as much again. But love your enemies, and do good, and lend, expecting nothing in return; and your reward will be great, and you will be sons of the Most High; for he is kind to the ungrateful and the selfish. Be merciful, even as your Father is merciful.

In this passage the Lord exhorts us to extend our love to those who don't love us, who are ungrateful and selfish. Even sinners love those who love them. There is no inherent virtue in returning good for good. Every day we come across many unlovable, ungrateful, and unfriendly individuals that we are commanded to love and forgive.

The story is told of a missionary who served a colony of people with leprosy. His aim was to bring the gospel to the least loved and most-universally shunned people in the world. One patient met him every day with extreme hostility—yelling obscenely and flinging garbage at him. Despite this ongoing contempt, the missionary visited the man every day, until one afternoon, eighteen years later, he accepted Christ. Surely, the love of Christ extends to the most abject and resistant human being. Love can win them to his kingdom by its power and durability.

Most of us find it much easier to love Christians than others, though even Christians are not always easy to love. How instinctively we can react to the pettiness, selfishness, immorality, and disinterest of many of our contemporaries. How frequently those around us seem to take advantage, to offend or ignore us. In fact, more and more people in our society are behaving in decidedly unchristian ways. Such behavior can tax us well beyond our limits. Fortunately, we can rely on the power of God to love others, regardless of how unloving they might act. Our decision to love and serve difficult people must remain firm. God's grace makes loving action possible. Jesus' own example is one of unfailing love. Richard Wurmbrand graphically recounts the torture he underwent in the communist prison camps of Rumania. But he repeatedly cites the power of Christ's love alive in the most desperate and challenging circumstances:

> We know about the love of Christ toward the communists by our own love toward them.
> I have seen Christians in communist prisons with 50 pounds of chains on their feet, tortured with red-hot iron pokers, in whose throats spoonfuls of salt had been forced, being kept afterward without water, starving, whipped, suffering from cold, and praying with fervor for the communists. This is humanly inexplicable! It is the love of Christ, which was shed into our hearts.[5]

Another account emphasizes the converting power of Christian love toward those who seem impossible to love,

> A Christian was sentenced to death. Before being executed, he was allowed to see his wife.

His last words to his wife were, *"You must know that I die loving those who kill me. They don't know what they do and my last request of you is to love them, too. Don't have bitterness in your heart because they kill your beloved one. We will meet in heaven."* These words impressed the officer of the secret police who attended the discussion between the two. Afterward he told me the story in prison, where he had been put for becoming a Christian.[6]

By witnessing the heroic love of numerous Christians for their tormenters, Wurmbrand concludes:

God will not judge us according to how much we endured, but how much we could love. I am a witness for the Christians in communist prisons that they could love. They could love God and men.[7]

We can receive inspiration from these extraordinary accounts as we seek to love and do good to more ordinary sinners in more ordinary daily circumstances. For most of us, determined love will probably take more modest forms:

—continuing to be courteous to an inconsiderate neighbor

—forbearing our employer's sarcasm and partic-

ularly demonstrating appropriate respect
—doing a favor for a critical, ungrateful in-law
—regularly visiting an invalid aunt who endlessly
  details her sufferings,
—giving a small gift to a stingy co-worker
—volunteering to cut the lawn of our unfriendly,
  vacationing neighbor

I was once praying with great fervor for the conversion of a friend, when the Holy Spirit interrupted me with this practical directive: "Go wash his car. You can pray at the same time."

We can find many occasions to love others— without expecting a return. Giving a helping hand, buying a lunch, offering a car ride, loaning a tool, baking a dessert—there are innumerable opportunities to give and do good. These kind of actions warm and win the hearts of others.

One Christian family I know makes it a practice to welcome newcomers into their neighborhood. They not only introduce themselves, but offer practical assistance as well. The husband and his sons try to pitch in with some of the heavy work; the wife makes a meal or two. This kind of help prepares the soil of their hearts for later spiritual influence.

My neighborhood has many Christians living it. We have tried to take a concern for loving and serving our non-Christian neighbors.

My wife, for instance, recently co-hosted with

her Christian friends, a tea for a new mother on the street. The women had a great time together. The focus was not at all spiritual, but social. The women were being loved and served in a way that they could experience as such.

Opportunities to serve come up frequently in the neighborhood. One warm Saturday, our neighbor across the street began digging up a section of his lawn in order to pour a new driveway extension. I noticed that Tony, my Christian neighbor, joined him with his shovel. Shortly after, I joined them. We put in a couple hours, voluntarily and spontaneously, and reduced an all day, one-man job to a few hours.

If we are eager to win people for Christ, we should likewise be eager to love and serve them. In these acts of generosity, Christ is speaking to them: "I love you. You are important to me. I care about your needs."

We should be led by the Holy Spirit and his wisdom in serving others. It would be imprudent, for instance, to so aggressively serve outsiders that we neglect some of our basic responsibilities. We cannot meet every need or serve every person we meet. A Christian is not just an indiscriminating do-gooder, but one who thoughtfully seeks to advance the kingdom of God through his works of charity.

On the other hand, we should not do good

simply for the sake of evangelizing others. "OK, now I shovelled your sidewalk, come to my Bible study!" Our temptation can be to serve expecting a harvest, thus reducing our inclination to serve others unless there is the possibility of evangelistic fruit. We should determinedly love, do good, and lend, and not just for the sake of evangelizing.

When saying that our "reward will be great," Jesus is giving us great incentive for loving all men. "Give and it will be given to you; good measure, pressed down, shaken together, running over, will be put into your lap" (Lk 6:38). The single reward stated by Jesus is that we will become more and more like God our Father. We shall see God. One day we will be united with him forever.

I have heard countless individuals attest to how their lives had been changed through Christian charity and mercy. Those who experience Christian love and service are hearing a message much like the glory of God described in the heavens:

> The heavens are telling the glory of God;
>   and the firmament proclaims his handiwork.
> Day to day pours forth speech,
>   and night to night declares knowledge.
> There is no speech, nor are there words;
>   their voice is not heard;

Yet their voice goes out through all the earth,
and their words to the end of the world.
(Ps 19:1-4)

If we are to be effective ambassadors of Christ,
we must affirm our message with action, season-
ing the world with salt and brightening it with
light.

EIGHT

Earning the Right to Be Heard

EXCELLENCY IN CHARACTER and conduct should be the trademark of every disciple of Jesus Christ. Jesus himself, fully man and fully God, was perfect in all that he said and did. He was God's example to us of peerless character—a man of courage, faithfulness, integrity, obedience, and loyalty. He conducted himself so that all who heard him listened. The crowds "were astonished at his teaching, for he taught them as one who had authority, and not as their scribes" (Mt 8:28b-29). Jesus earned "the right to be heard."

We, too, must earn the right to be heard. If our lives fall short under the scrutiny of a watchful observer, that same observer will be more apt to dismiss any spiritual message we might impart. On the other hand, if we demonstrate excellency of conduct and speech in our daily relationships, people will listen more seriously to what we have to say about the Christian life. Our message will be credible. Credible is defined as "worthy of belief; trustworthy; reliable; entitled to confidence." This kind of credibility accounted for the evangelistic success of Christ's infant church: "And day by day, attending the temple together and breaking bread in their homes, they partook of food with glad and generous hearts, praising God and having favor with all the people. And the Lord added to their number day by day those who were being saved." (Acts 2:46-47)

The leader of that early church, Peter, later instructed the Christians regarding the effective witness. "Maintain good conduct among the Gentiles, so that in case they speak against you as wrongdoers, they may see your good deeds and glorify God on the day of visitation" (1 Pt 2:12).

Similarly, the apostle Paul says to the church at Thessalonica: "We exhort you brethren . . . to aspire to live quietly, to mind your own affairs, and to work with your hands, as we charged you; *so that you may command the respect of outsiders,* and be dependent on nobody" (1 Thes 4:11-12).

Both Peter and Paul, great giants of the faith, emphasize the importance of the witness of a Christian life to outsiders. Every group that is interested in promoting a message or vision for life perceives how important their members' conduct is. Many of us have heard of the Boy Scout law, the list of qualities that should characterize a scout. A scout is: trustworthy, loyal, helpful, friendly, courteous, kind, obedient, cheerful, thrifty, brave, clean, reverent.

Peter supplies us with God's list of qualities in 2 Peter 1:5-8:

> For this very reason make every effort to supplement your faith with virtue, and virtue with knowledge, and knowledge with self-control, and self-control with steadfastness, and steadfastness with godliness, and godliness with brotherly affection, and brotherly affection with love. For if these things are yours and abound, they keep you from being ineffective or unfruitful in the knowledge of our Lord Jesus Christ.

The Lord wants us to be the kind of people who command the respect of others. We should be known as responsible and self-controlled people. Our word should be reliable. We should be able to be counted on. If we are not, our verbal witness will count for little.

Two cases in point illustrate the necessity of good conduct, one negatively and one positively.

A Christian college student by the name of Joe plays varsity basketball. He is especially known for his Christian commitment and aggressive evangelism. He talks to other players about following the Lord and uses every opportunity to give his testimony. As a matter of fact, his speech is always peppered with "Praise the Lord" and "Alleluia" in practices and games. Beside this, he is an excellent ballplayer who starts in every game.

One might think, given this description, that Joe is sowing some spiritual seed that will bear fruit. Unfortunately, this isn't the case. Joe is known, not only for his fervor and talent, but also for his unreliability. He is usually late for practice and sometimes late for games. He can't be counted on in the normal rigors of preparation and is sloppy with his schoolwork. As far as discipline and responsibility go, Joe is manifestly deficient, and this shortcoming costs him severely whenever he tries to witness for Christ. Because of his obvious unreliability Joe might, in fact, be doing the gospel more harm than good. Though zealous and well intentioned, Joe has failed to earn the respect of his peers and coaches.

Just as poor conduct undermines verbal witness, excellent conduct promotes evangelistic success. Larry is a local businessman who has helped many of his associates draw closer to the Lord. As aggressive in his verbal witnessing as Joe, Larry concentrates even more on his behavior in the office and in general. He is not only competent in his professional duties, but reliable, respectful, and cooperative as well. Because he is so respected, others give weight to his Christian convictions and are postively influenced. Larry recently showed me a letter of recommendation his boss wrote for him:

> I have had the pleasure of professional association with Mr. Jenkins for the past five years. In all my dealings with him, I have found him to be both fair and uncompromising in principle. His work is always of the highest calibre. Reliability is his trademark.
>
> Both clients and co-workers respect him, and, as his supervisor, I too, hold him in high regard. I unreservedly recommend him in his area of expertise. In my frank opinion, he is a fine Christian gentleman.

It is worth noting that Larry's boss is not a Christian. However, his respect for Christianity has grown through his association and regard for Larry. He even mentions Larry's Christianity favorably in his letter of recommendation.

The respect and credibility we command through our actions and reputation can help us to assess how verbally aggressive we should be with the gospel. Larry's verbal witness was effective because his life visibly reinforced his convictions. Joe's verbal witness, backfired because of his shortcomings. Joe should have taken steps to grow in responsibility. At the same time, he should have been more discreet in his preaching.

Though strength of character is important, I am not asserting that we must be perfect before we proclaim Christ. However, the better we are as persons, the more powerful our proclamation. In certain relationships, where we are particularly prone to error, we might wisely decide to subdue our verbal witness. We should not strain our effectiveness beyond its limits. Conversely, in situations where we have established a good reputation, we can and should be telling others about our relationship with the Lord. Whenever possible, we should take maximum advantage of our good reputation.

We should regularly and prayerfully appraise the quality of our conduct. Who are the people we often relate to? Are we respected among them? Do our neighbors know us as reliable and courteous? Are we patient and thoughtful with our roommate? Do we need to apologize for any wrongdoing we have committed in our family? How can we improve our behavior on the job?

This kind of assessment will not only help us improve our witness, but will give us wisdom in assessing how actively we should speak of Christ in various relationships (Col 4:5).

For those who work outside the home, the quality of our work will play a major influence in our ability to evangelize others at the workplace.

Scripture offers wisdom for those under forced employment (slaves) that can be helpful for the Christian employee today. I am certainly not suggesting that we should conduct ourselves like Christian slaves on the job, but there is a rough analogy here. In Colossians 3:22-24 we read:

> Slaves, obey in everything those who are your earthly masters, not with eyeservice, as men-pleasers, but in singleness of heart, fearing the Lord. Whatever your task, work heartily, as serving the Lord and not man, knowing that from the Lord you will receive the inheritance as your reward; you are serving the Lord Christ.

These instructions are both clear and applicable.

Obey in everything. Many employees set their own standards for obeying their supervisors. The Christian should be committed from the heart, even when no one will see, to obey his boss in everything related to his work, unless it is sinful.

Not as man-pleasers, but God-pleasers. The Christian should not be primarily motivated by the attention he will get from his employer. His motive should be to please God.

In singleness of heart, fearing the Lord. The motive of the Christian worker is pure and generated by the fear of the Lord—not the fear of the annual performance review or the opinion of others.

Whatever your task, serve heartily. A recent report in a national news magazine cited widespread corruption in the world of work. Tax evasion, theft, sloth, graft, and wasting time were described as rampant features in small and large corporations. Consider how brightly a hardworking Christian shines in this atmosphere of increasing greed and laziness.

Having favor with both God and man is instrumental in spreading the gospel. The key to godly character of course, is God himself. Not only can we accomplish nothing without him— we can *be* nothing without him. It is his power within us that enables us to be more than conquerors—victors over our own personal deficiencies and winners of men as well.

NINE

Speaking about Christ

COMMUNICATING SPIRITUAL TRUTHS in our natural settings, can be a great challenge. Sometimes our attempts result in embarrassment.

I remember a job I held years ago. I was eager to use every opportunity to tell others about my relationship with the Lord. In the absence of natural opportunity, I sometimes engineered illfated conversations about spiritual subjects.

One of these took place one day with a coworker named John. Poor John desperately needed to hear the gospel, though he didn't know it. He was recently divorced, involved in another relationship, and anxiety ridden about his career. If only someone spiritual like me could open the gates of heaven for John!

The right moment never seemed to come as my eagerness to talk to John brewed nearly to a boiling point. Finally, one day, I attempted a spiritual ambush. In the midst of a pleasant conversation, I made my move:

John (with some anxiety): "I've got to find a new job. I'm really at a dead end here in this place. I need more money."

Jim (in a crouch position): Well John, life is really just a mist. Before you know it we'll all be gone, jobs and all." (I refrained from citing Psalm 90 as a reference.)

John (ending the conversation with indignation): "Well, that sure is a religious statement if I ever heard one!"

Somehow, the spiritual relevance of my comment escaped John and practically ended any chance I had to reach him with the message of salvation.

My comment to John backfired for at least two reasons. First, I was impatiently manipulating the conversation. Second, my pious comment smacked of an impersonal religiosity that didn't speak to his expressed concern.

When speaking about Christ, spiritual truths, our prayer group, community, or church, we need wisdom as well as zeal. Wisdom should be our guide in communicating effectively about the Lord's life to outsiders. "Conduct yourselves wisely toward outsiders, making the most of the time. Let your speech always be gracious, seasoned with salt, so that you know how you ought to answer everyone." (Col 4:5-6)

This passage cites wisdom and discretion as key ingredients in effective communication. Discretion demands our alertness not only to the person but to the situation. Though my comment to John was true enough, it was not sensitively geared to the overall conversation. "A word fitly spoken is like apples of gold in a setting of silver" (Pr 25:11). "To make an apt answer is a joy to a man, and a word in season, how good it is!" (Pr 15:23).

Speak Simply

An ex-marine once told me of a frequently used abbreviation in the corps—KISS.

"That's interesting," I countered, "What does KISS mean?" "Keep It Simple Stupid," he replied. For our purposes, let me substitute: "Keep It Simple Saint."

Everyone appreciates simplicity of communication. We need not be complex or theological as we talk about the Lord. We don't need to overpower our hearers in a torrent of words.

Speak Personally and Sincerely

The apostle Paul was a great preacher to both Jew and Gentile. Yet he was remarkably and consistently personal in transmitting the gospel. He uses many situations to give his personal testimony in the record of the Acts of the Apostles. Even in the midst of his eloquent defense before King Agrippa in Caesarea, he presents his personal story. Agrippa responds by saying, "In a short time you think to make me a Christian!"

Likewise, it is usually best to speak personally about our own relationship with the Lord and his people. The hot air of theological debate can be quickly deflated with personal reference to the Lord. Tell people how God has worked concretely in your life—answering prayers, giving guidance, changing your marriage, easing your problems, strengthening your character, providing for your financial needs.

Avoid False Piety

We should diligently avoid jargon that sounds strange to unchurched ears: "Praise God, I was really blessed and edified!" "If it weren't for the fellowship and the blood, I'd be a backslider." "Let me tell you about life in the body." "For the grace of God that bringeth salvation hath appeared to all men." These and similar sounding phrases can alienate men and women.

If our speech is to be seasoned with salt, we should realize that much Christian jargon is not only perplexing but often offensive to outsiders. Within decent bounds (that is, righteous and appropriate), our speech should fit into the given environment.

Christians can also use jargon which is not necessarily religious sounding but which is unique to their church or fellowship, and thus meaningless to outsiders. Although I am a "coordinator" in "The Word of God," an inter-denominational Christian community, I describe myself to others as one of the directors of a Christian organization. We should be careful to avoid jargon, especially when talking to outsiders. This advice proceeds from the scriptural recommendations to "be all things to all men."

Don't Be Moralistic and Pushy

One of the surest ways to alienate non-Christians is to confront them about their morals. They will respond defensively, and you will simply be reinforcing the widely held misconception that Christianity is primarily a moral code. While morality is of critical importance, moralizing is most often harmful, particularly to those who have never heard the good news.

I know a young man who was involved in serious wrong at the time of his conversion. In ignorance, he continued in this wrongdoing until another Christian gently educated him in the matter. He immediately changed his behavior, motivated by his desire to live completely for God. It is normally only this motivation plus the operation of God's power that can produce such moral change. Without these two bases, moralizing will most normally provoke resistance and defensiveness.

Likewise, pushiness usually provokes mistrust and reluctance. Take the case of Carl. A successful student and star athlete, he was nonetheless disenchanted with his life and was looking for a spiritual solution to his problems. As he came into contact with some Christians on campus, he was keenly interested but cautious about expressing commitment. Encouraged by Carl's interest, but failing to note his uncertainty, a Christian worker doggedly pressed Carl for a commitment, only to lose him completely. Had that Christian exercised patient faith and greater sensitivity, Carl might well have taken the needed step.

As servants of the Lord, we must always be attentive to the initiative of the Master. No one can come to the Father except by the Son. No one can come to the Son unless the Father calls him. Placing our trust in the action of God in others can often be a great challenge for a fervent, well intentioned Christian ambassador. Without faith however, our work will be to no avail. As we exercise patient faith for others, we will see results.

This is not to say that we shouldn't urge or gently push at the right moment. Nor should we be tepid and indecisive in calling others on to the Christian life. The important point is to be sensitive both to the person and the work of the Holy Spirit in the other person. A Spirit filled push at the right moment can be just what's needed.

Guard Your Tongue

Complaining and criticalness come naturally to human beings. Our society encourages us to evaluate and criticize everyone and everything. Politicians, ministers, foreigners, neighbors, relatives, spouses, bureaucrats in Washington, barbers, socialists, capitalists—everyone is a target for criticism and slander.

In this atmosphere of negativity the command of Jesus rings out unmistakably: "Judge not, that you not be judged" (Mt 7:1). The Christian who faithfully obeys this command refuses to follow the crowd. Christians should not judge and criticize others, except in cases where they have responsibility over people or situations. Even then, their judgment should be objective and merciful.

The inclination to find fault with others can seem overpowering. It's easy to see how others fall short. But what are we conveying when we openly criticize others? If nothing else, a criticizing Christian demonstrates that he or she is no different than anyone else, no light on a hilltop, no lamp on a stand.

One cannot overestimate the positive impact of speech that is uncontaminated by slander and meanness. I know a number of individuals who were initially drawn to Christ through witnessing the positive attitude and speech of Christians. This was a trait that impressed me before I fully encountered Lord. I would even attempt to draw Christians into a negative conversation and then marvel at their resistance. I found their behavior mystifying and irritating at the same time. What strange view of reality could support such positive attitudes and speech? If the Christians around me had spoken like the rest of my contemporaries, I probably wouldn't have been very curious about Christianity.

Never underestimate the power of the tongue—for great good, or great evil. Christians should "speak evil of no one" (Ti 3:2a).

Finally, for the sake of both righteousness and witness, we should avoid criticism of other Christians or Christian groups. Would not an outsider conclude "See how those Christians hate one another!" The current scandal of division among Christians should greatly motivate us to speak well, or not at all, of our brethren.

Be Gentle and Courteous

Three striking phrases follow on the heels of Paul's recommendation "to avoid quarreling, to be gentle, and to show perfect courtesy toward all men" (Ti 3:2). This might strike us as ill-suited advice from someone who seemed to thrive on debate, as the apostle Paul. His strong verbal defense of the gospel always occurred in contexts where debate was socially acceptable. Moreover, Paul repeatedly demonstrated courtesy and meekness in his dealings with both Jew and Gentile. His immediate apology for a harsh and ill-informed rebuke to Ananias the high priest, is a striking example of Paul's allegiance to his own teaching (Acts 23:1-5).

Paul's interest in gentleness and courtesy is due to his interest in evangelism. In 2 Timothy 2:24-25 he states: "And the Lord's servant must not be quarrelsome but kindly to everyone . . . forbearing, correcting his opponents with gentleness. God may perhaps grant that they will repent and come to know the truth."

Peter shows a similar concern to instruct his listeners in discreet speech: "Always be prepared to make a defense to anyone who calls you to account for the hope that is in you, yet do it with gentleness and reverence" (1 Pt 3:15).

Both Peter and Paul highlight the value of courtesy, gentleness, and reverence in speech. Interestingly, they correlate these qualities with evangelism. Sidestepping futile arguments and avoiding a quarrelsome tone is stressed in a number of passages regarding speaking with outsiders. Non-Christians will frequently try to provoke and draw a Christian into similarly obnoxious behavior. It is essential for us to overcome such a temptation if we are to communicate the truth about Christ. The manner in which we speak is normally as closely scrutinized as our words themselves. We can still speak softly, knowing that we are, indeed, carrying a big stick.

The above six recommendations cite both how we should and should not speak about the Christian life to those who are not Christians. They recognize certain tendencies of the tongue and errors into which we can readily fall. It is perilously easy to commit any or all of the six errors mentioned. With ease, we may find ourselves:

1. presenting the gospel in a complicated or confusing manner
2. speaking impersonally, theologically
3. using religious jargon
4. pushing when we shouldn't
5. criticizing others
6. running roughshod over people, being defensive and insensitive.

If you can relate to any of these tendencies, don't be disheartened! Though we are filled with the Spirit of God, we are still hampered by our imperfect human tendencies. As we master the tongue, we will not only be more pleasing to God but to outsiders as well.

TEN

Authentic Evangelism

IS THE JOB OF EVANGELISM COMPLETED once an individual has made a commitment to Jesus Christ? Not if we take seriously the teaching of Jesus about the kingdom of God.

Jesus Christ came among men preaching the kingdom of God. Now this phrase "the kingdom of God" sounds strange to modern ears. Nevertheless, we should understand what Jesus meant by this kingdom. When the people of Galilee begged him to stay with them, he replied by saying, "I must preach the kingdom of God to the other cities also; for I was sent for this purpose" (Lk 4:43). Later, Luke records that "he went on through cities and villages, preaching and bringing the good news of the kingdom of God" (Lk 8:1). There are literally scores of references to this kingdom cited throughout the Old and New Testaments.

Just what is this kingdom? On earth it is that human society which has come under the reign of Jesus Christ. The kingdom then, is a society of believers under the reign of God awaiting its full establishment at Christ's return. This redeemed society is distinct from the kingdom of this world, the other human society where Jesus is not acknowledged as Lord.

Jesus' intention in evangelism is not simply to redeem individuals (though this is crucial) but to incorporate them, into a transformed community. It is within the body of Christ that believers are brought to maturity and fruitfulness. Together, their lives give witness to the world that Jesus is Lord, extending his influence to bring others into that same new life. "He has delivered us from the dominion of darkness and transferred us to the kingdom of his beloved Son" (Col 1:13). Peter highlights this fact also: "But you are a chosen race, a royal priesthood, a holy nation, God's own people that you may declare the wonderful deeds of him who called you out of darkness into his marvellous light" (1 Pt 2:9).

God wants to win others to himself *through* his kingdom and *into* his kingdom. This is the basis upon which to understand our personal involvement in evangelism: A widely accepted misunderstanding of the gospel undercuts God's full intention with evangelism. One might refer to it as the abbreviated gospel. The inadequacy of this notion of the nature of the good news naturally leads to an understanding of evangelism that is highly individualized and short-sighted. It often limits the focus of personal witnessing to helping others make a verbal acceptance of Christ without emphasizing the ongoing need for commitment and relationship with other Christians. The fruit borne can be dramatic, but it is often woefully shortlived. Consider the following examples of this kind of approach:

—According to a recent Gallup poll 33 percent of adult Americans claim to have been born again. This is a startling statistic, indeed, when one considers the obvious realities of modern life. Statistics on divorce rates, sexual promiscuity, and widespread cheating in business and industry, fly in the face of the claim on the part of one out of every three adult Americans to have been born again. Where are these millions of Christians? Where is the evidence of their redemptive influence upon our post-Christian culture? Might they have died prematurely, withered on the vine?

—A man's dormitory in a nominal Christian university is visited one evening by a touring evangelistic troupe. Upon presenting the gospel message, the leader asks for commitment from the students, to be indicated by the raising of hands. Virtually all of the 200 students in attendance make this commitment to Christ. Publicized as one of its most notable evangelistic successes, the evangelistic group makes little or no effort to follow-up on these decisions. Satisfied that arm-lifting indicates conversion, the group is unaware that no observable change occurs in the lives of the students. Premarital sex and drunkeness continue to thrive in that particular dormitory.

—A nationally renowned entertainer claims conversion to Christ. After recording a hit song about the experience, he resumes his former blatantly decadent lifestyle.

—A professional athlete who is avowedly and publicly born-again divorces his wife, remarries, and divorces again.

One can think of countless examples of this kind of evangelism and its distorted Christian ideology. I remember leading a young man to Christ about ten years ago. As he prayed aloud his commitment, I thought, "Thank God, he crossed over." Because I had a stunted understanding of the gospel, I did not industriously help him to establish a prayer life, join a church, or improve his marriage. Six months later he admitted sadly, "You know, I asked God into my life and had a great momentary experience. But now I look back and see that my life is the same as before. I haven't changed at all."

Paul says: "Him we proclaim, warning every man and teaching every man in all /wisdom, that *we may present every man mature in Christ.* For this I toil, striving with all the energy which he mightily inspires within me" (Col 1:28-29).

Authentic evangelism is not completed when the message of salvation is verbally proclaimed. Neither has it fully succeeded when people respond with faith and commitment. These are crucial elements but more is needed to establish new believers in a productive and enduring Christian way of life.

I would suggest that we understand authentic evangelism as the process by which we, as members of a redeemed community, help others to establish, re-establish, or significantly deepen a personal relationship with Jesus Christ. The process of evangelism is not complete, however, until the individual is helped to take the crucial steps which promote and insure ongoing growth in the Christian life. This would include connection with some kind of vital, committed Christian fellowship.

We can see, then, that our goal in evangelism is not simply to help others make decisions for Christ or accept Christ as Lord although this is of absolute importance. Rather, it is to help them also to establish a basic Christian lifestyle that will be fruitful in years to come. We want to produce "fruit that will abide"—the kind of fruit that Jesus desires his disciples bear and that proves that they are his disciples. Like the great evangelist and apostle Paul, our vision for evangelism should be the full, uncondensed version: "Him we proclaim, warning every man and teaching every man in all wisdom, *that we may present every man mature in Christ.* For this I toil, striving with all the energy which he mightily inspires within me." (Col 1:28-29)

Paul toiled endlessly not just to verbally declare the gospel, but also for the full integration of that gospel into the lives of his converts. In other words, he was not satisfied with only a personal decision for Christ. *His aim was that the full life of Christ be worked out in each individual.*

This approach has many implications for our personal involvement in evangelism. First, it extends our responsibility and concern beyond mere verbal proclamation aimed to provoke a quick decision.

Second, it implies that we, as Christ's witnesses, can most effectively reach others if we are rooted in Christ and in solid Christian relationships. The more we evangelize out of the context of strong Christian relationships, the more effective we are in reaching others. Not only do we have more resources to rely on, but our own lives will witness to the joy of redeemed relationships. We can genuinely say to others, "Come and see."

Third, an accurate understanding of the full gospel message greatly increases our field of harvest. We are not only now considering these people who are avowedly non-Christian. Rather, our outreach includes the many thousands who perhaps profess Christ and yet are not solidly rooted or growing in Christ. *Our harvest could accurately include many of those born-again adults who have failed to grow to Christian maturity.* Evangelism then, can feasibly include anything from helping someone commit or recommit their life to Christ to introducing an isolated and weak Christian to a thriving Christian environment.

Our commission as Christians is thus both extensive and challenging. As members of the body of Christ, we are trying to bring others into the full life that Jesus alone can give. Within this supportive Christian environment, we can apply the principles of personal evangelism that will truly contribute to changing the world.

Portrait of the Christian Ambassador

THREE QUALITIES ARE ESSENTIAL for the Christian ambassador. When all is said and done, our success will largely be determined by our faith, our love of God, and our love for men and women.

Faith

The work of *evangelism depends primarily upon the action of God.* God is the One Creator and sustains the world. God himself who intervened in human history to save all men through the one man, Jesus Christ. He now lives in us through the Holy Spirit, whose power enables us to love and serve him. We enter into these realities through faith. *Faith is the key for us.* Faith in God and reliance upon his promises and power are essential for divine approval. We concur with the writer of Hebrews when he boldly declares that "without faith it is impossible to please him" (Heb 11:6a).

In our evangelistic endeavors, we, too, recognize with the psalmist that "Unless the Lord builds the house, those who build it labor in vain. Unless the Lord watches over the city, the watchman stays awake in vain" (Ps 127:1). "Unless the Lord," is the constant instinctive refrain of our hearts as we realize the immensity of our Christian commission, the meagerness of our abilities, and the immeasurable greatness of him who sends us forth. With the psalmist we can say, "Some boast of chariots, and some of horses but we boast in the name of the Lord our God" (Ps 20:7). In this battle we do not trust in our bow, nor can our sword save us for "In God we have boasted continually" (Ps 44:8a).

As we serve the Lord in evangelism, we labor by faith in him. Though we gain insight and expertise through experience, our ultimate trust is founded in the work of his own hand with the people we are serving. One of the foremost principles for fruitful evangelism is to *pay first concern to what God seems to be initiating in someone's life and then to cooperate with that lead*. Such action is founded primarily in faith.

It is by *faith* that we decide to reach out to others. It is by faith that we are open about our Christian lives, that we invite friends and neighbors to share our lives, that we pray for them and take concern for them. By faith, too, we share the gospel with them, realizing that God's word will change lives. Paul rejoiced that his disciples in the city of Thessalonica first responded to his words because they recognized God's voice. "And we also thank God constantly for this, that when you received the word of God which you heard from us, you accepted it not as the word of men but as what it really is, the word of God, which is at work in you believers" (1 Thes 2:13). Again, Paul emphasizes that God gave the growth in Corinth, even though Paul planted and Apollos watered. "So neither he who plants nor he who waters is anything, but only God who gives the growth" (1 Cor 3:7).

Exercising faith for those around us can be challenging, particularly in light of some of the painfully obvious obstacles that prevent their spiritual progress. However, one of Satan's primary strategies to make us ineffective is to discourage and dishearten us. He will bring to our mind all the things that seemingly cannot be overcome. If we focus solely on the obstacles, our confidence will plummet. Here is precisely where faith begins. By its very nature faith focuses not on what is seen, but on what is invisible. *"Now faith is the assurance of things hoped for, the conviction of things not seen" (Heb 11:16).* As we work with and pray for those who haven't fully responded to God's call, we should view them with the imagination of faith. We should visualize them in our minds' eye precisely as God would have them be, not as they currently appear to be.

Trusting in God and knowing that our labor is not in vain releases God's power and enables his servants to work in his peace.

Love of God

Hear, O Israel: The Lord our God is one Lord and you shall love the Lord your God with all your heart, and with all your soul, and with all your might. (Dt 6:9)

And one of them, a lawyer, asked him a question, to test him. "Teacher, which is the great commandment in the law?" And he said to him, "You shall love the Lord your God with all your heart, and with all your soul, and with all your mind. This is the great and first commandment. (Mt 22:35-38)

Loving God wholly is the ultimate Christian ideal. It is why we were made. Our love for and pursuit of God will fuel our desire to see all people know and follow him.

It is no coincidence that the great evangelists through the ages have always demonstrated a sincere and loving devotion to God himself. This supreme love for Jesus Christ was the foundation for their evangelistic success. Likewise, we must root our evangelism within the context of our decision to love God above everything.

Anyone who would introduce Christ to another must first know Christ well himself. Anyone who would teach another to love Christ must love Christ first himself. The better one knows and loves his master, the more eager and competent he will be to show others the way.

As we direct every dimension of our lives toward loving and serving Jesus, we will, in fact, be increasingly eager to see his will done on earth. We will view those around us with God's eternal perspective, rather than with our own limited view. As we deepen our contact with the living God, we will bring his wisdom, charity, and courage to bear in our daily situations. *The more we love him, the more we will bear his image and likeness,* his interests and strengths, his perception and concern. We will see others with his eyes and respond to them with his mercy.

To love the Lord with all our hearts is not a romantic aspiration that provokes primarily an emotional response. It is a decisive commitment to a commandment which should mobilize all our energies and resources. The response is practical, as we seek to surrender our time, money, desires, and relationships to the will and good pleasure of our Maker. To fulfill the commandment requires our allegiance to the person who stands behind it and dependence on his grace to see it realized.

As we love God in prayer, in the reading of his word, and in service, we will grow in the fruit of the Spirit. A fruit tree with deep roots, that is regularly pruned and nourished, bears the most attractive fruit. Likewise, just as we have received Christ Jesus the Lord, so we should "live in him, rooted and built up in him and established in the faith." (Col 2:7). The fruit of the Spirit amply demonstrated in the life of a believer serves as an almost irresistable attraction to others. People want to be around and to be like one who embodies love, joy, peace, patience, kindness, goodness, faithfulness, gentleness, and self-control (see Gal 5:22-23). Such a person will draw others to Christ. We can demonstrate these qualities of character only to the degree that we are united to Christ.

Loving Others

The commandments, "You shall not commit adultery, you shall not kill, you shall not steal, you shall not covet and any other commandment, are summed up in this sentence, "You shall love your neighbor as yourself!"

(Rom 13:9)

For the whole law is fulfilled in one word, "You shall love your neighbor as yourself."

(Gal 5:14)

If you really fulfill the royal law, according to the scripture, "You shall love your neighbor as yourself" you do well. (Jas 2:8)

The third quality of the Christian ambassador is love for others. The dwelling of God is with man. Human beings are the focus of God's intense love and concern. God so loved us that he became like us in all things except sin. If the life of Christ shows us anything, it most dramatically and irrefutably proves God's love for men.

The second commandment sums up in seven words our obligation to others. This short phrase reflects remarkable psychological insight in directing us to love others as we love ourselves. All of us, by instinct, are concerned for our own need. Consider for a moment how thoroughly aware of our own needs we are. When we feel fatigue, hunger, or pain we eagerly seek relief. We are indignant when cheated, manipulated, violated, rejected by others. We go to great ends to make life work well for ourselves and to fulfill our aspirations and desires. The orientation to love ourselves comes quite naturally.

If we take but a fraction of this self-love and direct it toward the needs of others, we move in the direction commanded by the Lord. He wants us to become increasingly aware of the needs of others and to demonstrate a readiness to serve them. The Son of Man himself came not to serve, but to be served, and to offer his life for the ransom of many (Mk 10:45). Our charge is to carry the burdens of our neighbors and to view their needs with genuine concern.

Jesus cited the Good Samaritan as an ideal example of a person who, in his act of service to another human being, fulfilled the second commandment.

Jesus said: "A man was going down from Jerusalem to Jericho, when he fell into the hands of robbers. They stripped him of his clothes, beat him and went away, leaving him half dead. A priest happened to be going down the same road, and when he saw the man, he passed by on the other side. So, too, a Levite, when he came to the place and saw him, passed by on the other side. But a Samaritan, as he traveled, came where the man was; and when he saw him, he took pity on him. He went to him and bandaged his wounds, pouring on oil and wine. Then he put the man on his own donkey, took him to an inn and took care of him. The next day he took out two silver coins and gave them to the innkeeper. 'Look after him,' he said, 'and when I return I will reimburse you for any extra expense you may have.'

"Which of these three do you think was a neighbor to the man who fell into the hands of robbers?"

The expert in the law replied, "The one who had mercy on him."

Jesus told him, "Go and do likewise."

(Lk 10:30-37)

A brief analysis of the parable can alert us to loving others in our daily situations:

The Samaritan "as he traveled, came where the man was." The Samaritan was carrying out his own business when he came upon the man in distress. Likewise, we need not look around for all the needy people we can find in order to fulfill the commandment. *The Lord will provide sufficient opportunities in the course of our routine daily life*.

The parable says, "and when he saw him." The Samaritan perceived the man's awful condition. May we too perceive the miserable condition of our fellow men and woman. May we have eyes to see those around us who are ravaged by Satan, dying in sin, at the mercy of their circumstances. The first step in loving others as ourselves is simply to *see them* as they truly are.

The Samaritan "took pity on him." His immediate response was pity. He wasn't revulsed by the bleeding body, as perhaps the Levite had been.

He wasn't indifferent as perhaps the priest was. He responded with compassion. As we see the truly pathetic state of many around us, our response should be the same. It is this attitude which will give birth to appropriate action.

The Samaritan "went to him." He took initiative. Unlike the priest and Levite who sidestepped the problem, the Samaritan faced it squarely. His pity translated into action and involvement. Likewise, we are called to respond to people and reach out toward them. We should take initiative rather than shrinking back in fear or timidity.

He "bandaged his wounds, pouring out oil and wine. Then he put the man on his own donkey, took him to an inn and took care of him." What a beautiful description of personal service rendered at the cost of personal inconvenience, possessions, and time! With his own hands, cloth, wine, and oil the Samaritan helped the victim. The scripture says that the Samaritan loaded *his own* donkey with the bruised body. He further cared for him at an inn. Surely our love for others will normally carry a personal price tag.

"The next day he took out two silver coins and gave them to the innkeeper. 'Look after him,' he said, 'and when I return, I will reimburse you for any extra expense you may have.'" The Samaritan continued to serve at his personal expense and he had enough concern to follow up by insuring for the man's proper care until his full recovery. He showed a readiness to serve beyond the immediate need. His commitment to the man was genuine and deep, not merely functional. It proceeded from a heart that reflected the intention of God.

As Christian witnesses, we, too, must have a genuine interest in the welfare of others. This compassion and readiness to serve people is essential for effective evangelism. Watchman Nee, a twentieth-century Chinese teacher and martyr, underscored this principle in an address on evangelism and love for men:

> If you try to preach the gospel to the unsaved, but have never been touched by the words "God created man," so that you approach men as your fellows; if you have never had more than a casual interest in men; then you are unfit to preach Christ as "a ransom for many." It needs to dawn on us that God created man in His likeness and set His love on man because man was exceedingly precious to Him. *Unless man becomes the object of our affection we cannot possibly become a servant of men.* . . .
>
> Brothers and Sisters, in the light of God's passionate concern for man, can you still regard your fellows with indifference? We shall be worthless in His service unless our hearts are enlarged and our horizon is widened. We need to see the value God has set

on man; we need to see the place of man in God's eternal purpose; we need to see the meaning of Christ's redemptive work. Without that, it is vain to imagine that you and I can ever have a share in the great work of God. How can anyone be used to save souls who does not love souls? If only this fundamental trouble of our lack of love for men can be solved, our many other difficulties in relation to men will vanish. We think some people are too ignorant and we think others are too hard, but these problems will cease to exist when our basic problem of lack of love for men has been dealt with. When we cease to stand on a pedestal and learn to take our place as men among fellow-men, then we shall no longer disdain any.[8]

As we grow in these attributes—faith, love of God, and love of neighbor, we will be increasingly useful to the Lord of the harvest. Methods amount to nothing without the Spirit and character of God as the foundation and power for our outreach. That comes with prayer and fellowship with the Spirit. May God grant us all the grace to be formed in his nature so that we may bear lasting fruit for him.

Notes

1. Michael Green, "Theology with Imagination," New Covenant vol. 2, number (5) October 1981, p.14
2. C.S. Lewis, The Magician's ..., New York Magazine 1962, p.19
3. Walter A. Elwell, ... (Wheaton, Illinois ... Books, 1979), p.??
4. Keith Miller, The ..., 1965, p.44
5. Richard Wurmbrand, Tortured for Christ (London: Diane Books ...)
6. Ibid, p.45
7. Ibid, p.41
8. Watchman Nee, ... (Washington ...), 1965, p.??